Multidisciplinarity

T0359042

In *Manifesto for an Independent Revolutionary Art* André Breton and Diego Rivera, under the effects of German fascism and Russian Stalinism in society, argued that art can only impact society and be revolutionary if it becomes independent of any social constructs.

Almost six decades later, in the rise of what became known as "relational aesthetics," the field of multidisciplinarity is expanding and many artistic projects for social change claim to be multidisciplinary. However, such projects show that we are still far from a broad discourse of multidisciplinarity. *Multidisciplinarity: Projects for Social Change in Art and Culture* takes a step towards a down-to-earth discussion of the relation between disciplinary discourses and grand narratives in three different projects, focusing mainly on its artistic, cultural, and management aspects. Indeed, drawing from the eclectic construction of these three multidisciplinary projects, this volume serves to bridge the gap between the theoretical debates of disciplinary discourses and the harshness of everyday life in communities where projects for social change are being implemented.

Presenting a panoptical view that places academic research side by side with daily life, *Multidisciplinarity: Projects for Social Change in Art and Culture* unveils the bigger picture of both projects and interdisciplinary discourses. This insightful volume will appeal to students and researchers interested in fields such as project management, multidisciplinarity, cultural studies and organisational studies.

Luísa Santos is Assistant Professor at the Faculty of Human Sciences of Universidade Católica Portuguesa, Lisbon, Portugal.

Complexity and Interdisciplinarity in Project Management

Series Editors: Steve Raue and Louis Klein

Modern project management needs more than tools for creating order and control. The traditional approach to project management works in stable and predictable environments. Yet, reality tells us that managing projects mostly means managing continual change of project constraints, social dynamics, uncertainty and increasing complexity. New fields need to be sourced to understand project management from a broader range of perspectives.

The purpose of this series is to explore new, interdisciplinary approaches and perspectives on complexity in project management, with a particular focus on projects, programmes and portfolio, the vehicles that are fundamental for everything from the delivery of new products or services, to the development of new business processes and the transformation of the organization itself.

The titles in this series narrate emerging approaches to project management research and practice from a variety of fields around arts, discourse theory and cultural studies. The aim is to extend our understanding, transfer and adoption of new research methodologies to encourage an interdisciplinary thinking and doing of project management in times of increasing complexity.

Shadow Working in Project Management
Joana Bértholo

Multidisciplinarity: Projects for Social Change in Art and Culture
Luísa Santos

Multidisciplinarity

Projects for Social Change in Art and Culture

Luísa Santos

Routledge
Taylor & Francis Group

LONDON AND NEW YORK

First published 2019
by Routledge

2 Park Square, Milton Park, Abingdon, Oxfordshire OX14 4RN
52 Vanderbilt Avenue, New York, NY 10017

Routledge is an imprint of the Taylor & Francis Group, an informa business

First issued in paperback 2020

British Library Cataloguing in Publication Data
A catalogue record for this book is available from the British Library

Library of Congress Cataloging in Publication Data
A catalog record has been requested for this book

ISBN: 978-1-4724-8313-3 (hbk)
ISBN: 978-0-367-58961-5 (pbk)

Typeset in Times New Roman
by Taylor & Francis Books

Contents

Figures

Acknowledgements

First and foremost I want to thank my Ph.D. advisor Dr. Louis Klein. It has been an honour to be a Ph.D. student in the frame of the first edition of the ICCPM (International Center for Complex Project Management) programme initiated by Dr. Louis Klein at the Humboldt Viadrina School of Governance. He has taught me, both consciously and unconsciously, how good research is done and how to think critically about my assumptions. I deeply and truly appreciate all his contributions of time, ideas, knowledge, and motivation to make my Ph.D. experience productive and stimulating.

I am also immensely grateful to Prof. Dr. Hartmut Schröder, who welcomed and believed in my research and always supported its progress along these years, with immense trust and generosity. The members of the ICCPM group have contributed immensely to my personal and professional time during the Ph.D. The group has been a source of good advice and collaboration, even over enormous geographical distances.

In regards to *Morrinho*, the central case study, I thank Sigrun Guggenberger for bringing my attention to it; she was the first person to make my research possible and I am immensely grateful to her. Chico Serra and Cilan Oliveira showed me *Morrinho* through their personal stories and experiences, always with a great generosity and I very much appreciated their enthusiasm and insightful answers as well as interesting questions.

For the scientific methodology, I am extremely grateful to Dr. David Boje who generously and enthusiastically shared his ideas and immense knowledge in narrative methods and storytelling. The possible role of art in society discussed in this dissertation would not have been possible in a thorough way without the support of Maria Lind who welcomed my proposal for a series of seminars about art projects for social change at Tensta Konsthall, in Stockholm, which brought together artists and researchers.

I gratefully acknowledge the funding source that made my Ph.D. work possible. I was fully funded by the FCT (Fundação para a Ciência e Tecnologia) Ph.D fellowship for the duration of my research.

Lastly, I would like to thank my family for all their unconditional love and encouragement. For my parents who have always supported me in all my pursuits, despite all difficulties. My always inspiring mother who constantly and persistently supported me and taught me to be an active citizen, despite my personal and professional choices. My father who tried so hard during his life to teach me the meaning of patience. For my always kind, supportive, encouraging, loving, and patient Zé Pedro whose faithful and unconditional help and immense trust, encouragement, and support during all stages of my Ph.D. turned into this book is so very much appreciated. Finally, for my son Pedro Afonso, for patiently and lovingly making me fully aware of what truly matters in life.

Preface

Projects for social change

Louis Klein

Multidisciplinarity is key! Success sends you into the excellence trap. The reward for good work is more work of the same kind. This is true for project management as for research and eventually for all professional and academic disciplines. More of the same produces more of the same. The learning curve of continuous improvement yields on the long run only marginal returns. The challenges a mature discipline is facing will not go away. And not only for project management the crucial challenge is complexity.

Scott's principles of observation show a way out. To any given observation, so the cybernetician and systems scientist Bernard Scott explains, there is, first, always a bigger picture, there is, second, always more detail, and there is, third, always an alternative perspective. Luisa Santos' book is all about alternative perspectives and their combination. She argues the case of overcoming complexity with multidisciplinarity for the case of successful social change projects.

Multidisciplinarity: Projects for Social Change in Art and Culture is the second book coming out of a larger research project exploring alternative perspectives on project management, the cross-cultural complex project management research project (CCCPM). Project management as a discipline and a practice has been challenged in many ways. The greatest challenge however has been the unnerving fact that up to two thirds of all projects fail. Especially the large, the mega projects fail. This can be looked at as an entrepreneurial risk, however if we look at mega projects in the public arena where tax payers' money is at stake the issue cannot be reduced to the business case. It has political implications.

In 2008 the International Centre for Complex Project Management (ICCPM) was founded and devoted to the challenges of mega projects in the public arena. The reference to complexity in projects hereby served as a token, a placeholder addressing the need for further research to understand the dynamics which violate budgets, schedules, and quality of those mega projects in the public arena. The culprits, so to speak, the usual suspects, endangering project success at the time were identified as complexity and people. They were the scapegoats. They had to carry the blame if you wanted to keep up the engineering-based success story of project management as a discipline and a practice.

The CCCPM research project was the first research project established by the ICCPM back in 2008. It was dedicated to learning more about complexity and people and especially about complexity around the human factor. Following Noel Tichy's TPC model which distinguishes three perspectives on social systems, a technical perspective (T), a political perspective (P), and a cultural perspective (C). These three perspectives are equally rated. And if we agree that an engineering-based technical approach to project management accounts for one third of those perspectives, two thirds are neglected. The CCCPM research project combines those two perspectives under the headline of social complexity. This addresses and acknowledges that in human inter-action we see dynamic interdependence. People rearrange and change their behaviour in reflection of the behaviour of other people, which in turn creates a feedback loop where other people adjust their behaviour according to our behaviour. This is the cybernetic notion of a causal loop. Or frankly, wherever people are involved there is complexity.

In the pursuit of social complexity the CCCPM research project started to explore alternative perspectives on project management. It turns to different disciplines and fields. Sociology, psychology, and linguistics as well as arts and choreography to name but a few, were chosen as scientific disciplines which focus on human behaviour. In fields like capacity building, community development, coaching, training, consulting, event management, dance, and curating we find projects focusing on projects in relation to individuals, groups, and organisations. Bringing together those disciplines and fields, cul-tural studies allowed for a broad enough canvas to encompass the very diverse research on complex project management. The department of cultural studies at the European University Viadrina in Frankfurt/Oder, Germany, and The European School of Governance, Berlin, Germany provided an academic hub for the CCCPM research project.

The actual CCCPM research project operated as an independent graduate school, comprising not less than twelve PhD projects at a time. CCCPM cre-ated a transdisciplinary community of research with a critical exposure to aca-demic rigour. The various stages of the different research projects were brought forward in conferences and publications and eventually resulted in PhD theses which are brought forward here in this Routledge book series reaching out for a broader audience sharing insights and knowledge in pursuit of a next practice of project management which embraces complexity and people.

Multidisciplinarity: Projects for Social Change in Art and Culture is the second book out of the CCCPM research project. The first book *The Shadow of Project Management* by Joana Bértholo explored the implications of disciplinary rigour along the lines of Jungian psychology. Where there is light, there is shadow. Hence, project management as a discipline has a shadow, an unconscious side where all this dwells that had been ruled out. Joana Bértholo set out to meet the shadow and explored ways to acknowledge and integrate it into the discipline. Luisa Santos builds on this research but changes the direction of research to overcome the disciplinary shortcomings. Her path is multidisciplinarity.

Social change seems to be one of the great mysteries of our time. We all agree that social change is needed, however, there is little knowledge about how to bring about this change, let alone knowledge of robust and reliable methodologies to do so. On one side change is, so the bonmot, the only constant. On the other side, deliberate change comes in the form of a project. So, we better know something about project management. Yet, two thirds of all projects tend to fail. Complexity is the challenge and project management as we know it does not seem to do the trick. Creativity is needed and arts are regarded to be the stronghold of creativity. Hence, the prevailing idea is to foster social change based on what the arts can bring to the table. Be creative like an artist becomes an imperative and the rest is left to self-organisation. However, this approach fails as well. Self-organisation does not always yield desirable outcomes. Self-organisation like Adam Smith's invisible hand is not the hand of a benevolent god. It is just the description of systemic emergence, neither good nor bad. We cannot trust the invisible hand, we better watch it.

Luisa Santos starts, in the best of academic traditions, with a critical perspective on the pretentious claim of artistic social change projects to be viable change agents. She starts with the critical observation that the larger proportion of them fail. The analysis starts with a reflection on the arts acknowledging their character as social systems, social practice, and social sculpture. This leads to a bigger picture and more detail for the understanding of the potential and the limitations of the arts driving social change. In addition, Luisa Santos' initial analysis creates awareness for the cultural embedment of the arts and respectively for any social change project. Context matters and especially the cultural preconditioning of any human activity, be it arts or projects or change. Eventually, the analysis arrives at the understanding of social complexity in projects.

Two thirds of projects fail. The selection of the three case studies seems to reemphasise the statistics: First, Intervene: Heroes and Villains, second, Row Houses, and third, Morrinho. Two fail, one is a success. With the conceptual framework of her analysis Luisa Santos fosters a deeper understanding of success and failure of these three projects. Her findings open interesting pathways for deeper learning and promising knowledge transfer not only for social change projects, but for the issues of complexity in any kind of project.

Luisa Santos' work is full of research innovation. Out of this plenty two shall be highlighted. First is her very practical approach to multidisciplinarity which is not reduced to tap into multiple academic disciplines. Bravely and cunningly she combines three spheres which usually do not touch as disciplines, arts, academia, and management. While the various academic disciplines share a common logic, arts and management have their own logic, programmes, and paradigms. They are somehow alien to each other with all the difficulties to relate and communicate. And this is where Luisa Santos' second big research innovation facilitates progress.

All paradigms are communicated and processed in the form of narratives be it, like in this book, arts, academia, or management. Multidisciplinarity bridges the stories that make the world, stories of sense making and meaning creation. Multidisciplinarity explores paradigms and facilitates contact between strange worlds which can bring a lot to each other. As the mathematician Kurt Gödel proved, formal systems can yield questions that cannot be answered within these systems. And following Thomas Kuhn these are the questions which challenge and transform paradigms. Luisa Santos' work does not point at scientific revolutions. She facilitates the pragmatism of multidisciplinary learning. We do not need to reinvent the wheel if we can walk over to our neighbour who already produces carts.

Who should read this book?

This book is for you and me.

Projects are ubiquitous. They are everywhere. They serve our desire to get things done, to achieve our goals, to change and innovate. The research for "Projects for Social Change" started with the question of complexity, an invitation to project management. In the end, Luisa Santos' work on multidisciplinarity and projects addresses you and me.

This book is an invitation to a learning journey beyond project management, the book of knowledge, and the competence baselines. It meets the challenges beyond blueprints and Gantt charts. Like a good novel or a poem provides a language to share stories and narratives, this book enriches our ability to perceive the world differently. It provides a language to talk about these perceptions and share them; it allows us to embrace and overcome paradigms and the multitude of idiosyncratic disciplinary logics. This book prepares to meet the world beyond project management. You will learn more about the real world and the projects within it.

This book is a practical book for practitioners.

It addresses models, methods, and practices to find answers outside of project management or respectively outside your own disciplinary echo chamber. Thinking outside the box and learning to think without a box pave the way to probably not new but additional knowledge. Change starts with leaving the comfort zone. Disciplines and the according practices are comfort zones. It does not need a revolution to do old things differently and to engage in new practices. Continuous improvement and innovation can easily be fuelled by engaging with the world out there. We will find the answers if we allow ourselves to look for them in places which have not been on our map previously. Multidisciplinarity is key!

And finally, this book is for researchers.

It shows how multidisciplinarity and critical narrative theory allow for advanced qualitative research. They allow to bridge disciplines and strengthen the validity and robustness of research beyond triangulation. It is a common understanding that it is necessary to tap into at least three different research methods within a discipline to produce good research. Imagine what happens to the quality of research if triangulation reaches beyond the disciplinary boundaries. We may call it a new universe or just a new level of research innovation. It will certainly transform our understanding of research, our capabilities to meet complexity, and eventually our understanding of the world.

Dr Louis Klein is Dean at the SEUG and SIG chair for Organisational Transformation and Social Change.

Introducing projects for social change in art and culture

> True art, which is not content to play variations on ready-made models but rather insists on expressing the inner needs of man and of mankind in its time – true art is unable not to be revolutionary, not to aspire to a complete and radical reconstruction of society.
>
> *(Manifesto for an Independent Revolutionary Art,*
> Breton and Rivera, 1938)

In the *Manifesto for an Independent Revolutionary Art*, André Breton and Diego Rivera, under the effects of German fascism and Russian Stalinism in society, argued that art can only have an effect in society and be revolutionary if it becomes independent of any social constructs (Breton[1] and Rivera, 1938). Almost six decades later, in the rise of what became known as "relational aesthetics," a term devised by Nicolas Bourriaud in 1998, Dan Graham would write: "All artists are alike. They dream of doing something that's more social, more critical, and more real than art." This text was the caption of his work *Two-way Mirror Punched Steel Hedge Labyrinth* (1994), in the exhibition held at the Minneapolis Sculpture Garden, Walker Art Center, in Minneapolis, in 1998.

If we think of art as a social system – an idea coined by German sociologist Niklas Luhmann, in his seminal work from 1984 *Soziale Systeme: Grundriß einer allgemeinen Theorie*, that puts art in the domain of perception – we will understand art for what it does at its best: showing various realities, and ways to look at the world we live in, at social, economic, and political levels. In keeping with Luhmann's larger project, art, like the law, the economy, politics, or science, constitutes a specific social system of modernity. In other words, the specific semantic theme of art is the relationship between the non-social domain of conscious perception and the social domain of communication. The function of art would thus consist of integrating what is in principle incommunicable – namely, perception – into the communication network. Falling back on the total immersion in the discussions of the current situations, art operates in the production of images, objects, and whatever fits best a visual translation of such immersion.

In this process of immersion – emersion in the real, parts of the real will inevitably stay hidden. But it is precisely because of the critical distance implicit in this selective act that – as Martin Heidegger described in his search for the origin of the artwork in his 1977 book *Der Ursprung des Kunstwerkes* – it is possible to understand the world we live in.

Artists live the social, economic, and political changes and change with it. As co-founder of Culture+Conflict, Michaela Crimmin, has noted, most artists are not working in their close studios anymore: there are artists witnessing and participating in the everyday of war; artists who are social activists; artists who use their work as a way of communicating and addressing social change; artists asking for a wider participation from all citizens; artists who make critical observations; and artists who choose to be part of small and big revolutions (Crimmin and Stanton, 2014, p. 5).

The research presented here started precisely from the observation that an enormous and growing variety of artistic and cultural projects, usually but not exclusively initiated by artists, show a sustained interest in the human anxieties residing in the social and the political spheres of life.

Morrinho is a project aiming for social change, which shows a strong art focus but that involves other disciplines and might be regarded as multidisciplinary: the project aims to change the preconceived ideas (or perceptions) of what a favela might mean. However, when critically looking at this project, as well as other multidisciplinarity projects, it becomes clear that multidisciplinarity projects fighting preconceived ideas, mainly through art, show themselves to be preconceived ideas in disciplinary discourses. The other projects analysed in this text are *Project Row Houses* and *Intervene: Heroes and Villains*, both initiated in the 1990s, with a strong artistic focus, and aiming for social change, as *Morrinho*. The differences that each project shows in terms of geographic, social, economic, and cultural references inform a series of conclusions regarding the existing contexts of the projects as well as their aims and outcomes.

Art is a form of storytelling, and unlike many other disciplines, artists across art forms have the freedom to give a subjective account of the world we live in. Furthermore, there is no expectation of artists to make linear narratives with a conclusion. Rather than presenting us grand narratives of the world, the three projects under analysis greet us with small stories and voices that are usually silenced. This process of giving voice to small stories is mindful of what David Boje calls narrative methods (2007), the chosen research methodology of this study and one that has been used in project management and social sciences for the understanding of organisations. This methodology understands the power of narratives in unveiling reality. By acknowledging the existence of many narratives, such methodology exposes how history is very often made of grand narratives. In other words, how stories told by the powerful become one accepted History while the small stories told by many become silenced during this same History.

Narratives and storytelling are powerful analytical and methodological tools as the three projects presented in this study tell. *Morrinho, Project Row*

Houses and *Intervene: Heroes and Villains* sharply unveil grand narratives. On one hand, these grand narratives are opposed by the many small stories of people who have been silenced during History; on another hand, these grand narratives also appear linked to the histories of each discipline, with their attached and, sometimes, resolute ideas.

The disciplines under reading in these projects are art, cultural studies, and project management. All projects are initiated by artists (or by people who come to be seen as such, in the case of *Morrinho*); all aim to operate in the cultural domain of a specific group of people; and all are regarded as projects despite their understanding or professional skills of management to create a project from beginning to ending.

It seems that art, as a discipline, fears that scientific disciplines, as project management, take away the creative spark of a project. On another hand, it also seems that scientific disciplines look at art as a discipline incapable of working with specific goals and within a structured framework in tasks such as analysis of cultural references. This study shows that these assumptions do not hold the whole truth of the story and that each discipline, despite the sound knowledge in its specific field, has a strong tendency to be (partially) ignorant about the rest of the world.

An understanding of the true meanings – in opposition to preconceived ideas or grand narratives – of each discipline will, potentially, lead to results for the development of the execution of cultural and art-based projects for effective social change. We are still far from a broader discourse of multidisciplinary and future projects for social change can develop this approach. This will allow for fruitful integration and collaboration between disciplines that, alone, cannot produce effective social change. This multidisciplinary approach understands the importance of planning and strategy without dismissing creativity and the power of the individual.

When we – the audience – face *Morrinho, Project Row Houses* or *Intervene: Heroes and Villains*, we are invited to distance ourselves from what we think we know about the world and to enter the realm of interpretation in a method mindful of Bourriaud's relational aesthetics. This relational approach is crucial in the three projects as it allows for close identification with the subjects portrayed and tackled. Through this identification, the authors of the projects manage to get a direct response from the audience.

The direct contact required by an artwork (such as walking through the Lego figures holding guns that inhabit the 300-square metre model of Pereirão's favela which stands side by side with the actual favela) brings it to the reality of the here and now and implies social action from the audience. Such direct and physical contact is unique to art and, as Joseph Beuys famously claimed with his idea of "social sculpture,[2]" we all – as citizens, with different knowledge, skills, backgrounds, and contexts – have the creative potential to provoke collective reflections and actions for social change. It is precisely this collective responsibility that these three multidisciplinarity projects claim.

The story of a research in four chapters

The content of this book is developed and presented in the course of an Introduction, four chapters, and a series of final conclusions. After the introduction to the theme under study, Chapter 2 proposes a historiography, with a series of different interpretations of the proliferation of art and cultural projects for social change. This chapter intends to map various historical approaches and relationships between art and social change; cultural studies and social change; and, project management and social change.

In Chapter 3, in order to better understand and discover the reasons behind disciplinary grand narratives, art, cultural studies, and project management are analysed and unexpected inter-relationships – such as the ideas of creativity, chaos, and complexity – are unveiled. Here, it becomes clear that different disciplines use the same concepts and words but with different meanings, which points to problems of cultural translation.

Cultural translation comes up as an important issue in Chapter 3, while analysing three different multidisciplinary projects combining art, cultural studies, and project management for social change. *Intervene: Heroes and Villains* is a nine-month Portuguese project initiated by a museum in a so-called problematic community showing early-age school dropout but it seems that the project's team lacks a deep understanding of the community's history and cultural context. Artists and architects who regard themselves as activists initiated project Project Row Houses in Houston, Texas. Despite the good intentions, it appears that they have assumed they could overcome prejudice through an essentially formal intervention of art. *Morrinho* started off as a children's game and evolved into an NGO aiming for social change. It was initiated by and for the community, who soon became regarded as artists. It was then that they got a power that they had not experienced before.

Measuring the impact of artistic and cultural projects for social change is the endeavour of Chapter 4, which looks at the integration of art, cultural studies, and project management in multidisciplinarity projects for social change. In this chapter, each discipline shows its relevancy for their surprisingly shared characteristics such as creativity and complexity.

The book ends with conclusive thoughts on the contributions made by this research as well as opening up to a suggestion for future research. The research path has led to an unexpected answer: multidisciplinarity might be seen both as the solution – art alone might not be able to produce social change but together with other disciplines it seems to have a very significant role – and the problem – there are many misunderstandings and grand narratives associated with different disciplinary discourses making the communication between disciplines, sometimes, difficult. It seems that important work remains to be done in creating and working within a broader discourse of multidisciplinarity in projects for social change. With this unexpected conclusion, a proposal for linking the histories of art, cultural studies, and project management emerged as a possible path for a new and broader multidisciplinarity discourse.

Notes

1 It is believed that Trotsky and André Breton wrote the Manifesto, although Rivera and Breton signed it.
2 Social sculpture is a term coined by the German artist Joseph Beuys (1921–1986) through a series of public lectures in the early 1970s in America, which he named "Energy Plan for the Western Man." The term social sculpture was directed at a kind of artwork that takes place in the social realm, and, in order to be complete, would need social engagement and the participation of an audience (Kuoni, 1990). Beuys believed that as spectators became participants, the catalysis of social sculpture would lead to a transformation of society through the release of popular creativity. This term is more extensively presented in Chapter 2.

1 Historiography

The proliferation of art and cultural projects for social change

Art making is considered to be a universal human behaviour, which has always been a part of our personal and interpersonal communication (Malchiodi, 2007). In recent decades artists have gradually enlarged the boundaries of art, as they have wanted to engage with an increasingly pluralistic environment alternating between the everyday and the uncanny, the analytical and the critical. This pluralism of interests in art representations and interpretations shows the focus on critically observing and intervening in society and its culture as a point in common.

There are different perspectives regarding the History of Art in relation to social change. Whilst UNESCO asserts that what constitutes contemporary art has become dependent upon ideologies and political conflicts (UNESCO, 1977), art making has historically also been viewed as a means for exclusion (Bourdieu, 1984), and as a site that produces sociability in a relational way, mostly through engagement and participation (Bourriaud, 1998).

Many contemporary artists use their work with the intention to provoke responses both from the general audience, who, in the end, are citizens, and from the government. History has witnessed artists being arrested for their political positions; artists dealing with war; artists using art as propaganda; and artists who use their work as a trope to bring people together (Crimmin and Stanton, 2014).

In his book *Bad New Days: Art, Criticism, Emergency*, Hal Foster reflects on the importance of perception in acting in the world we live in. For Foster, the artists who constitute the avant-garde of today are the ones who take the formlessness of the "capitalist garbage bucket," with its undifferentiated proliferation of images and texts, and give it coherent form, making the precarious conditions of contemporary life tangible in a way that might point towards a different future. He puts his finger on the impossibility of art to change society on its own but points to what it can do very well: "take a stand...in a manner that brings together the aesthetic, the cognitive, and the critical in a precise constellation" (Foster, 2015). It is precisely in a series of constellations of multidisciplinarity discourses that social change seems to emerge.

Art as social system

There are different approaches, within the History of Art and Social Sciences, to understand art as a social system. This section looks at some of these various perspectives. These approaches show different views on the perception and goals that art might have in relation to society and how these goals and perceptions might (or might not) transform society.

In the 1938 *Manifesto for an Independent Revolutionary Art,* André Breton and Diego Rivera, seeing the consequences of German fascism and Russian Stalinism on society, argued that art could only have an effect on society and be revolutionary if it becomes independent of any social constructs. The Manifesto argued against the reactionary: "Independent revolutionary art must now gather its forces for the struggle against reactionary persecution. It must proclaim aloud the right to exist. Such a union of forces is the aim of the International Federation of Independent Revolutionary Art which we believe it is now necessary to form" (Breton and Rivera, 1938). Breton's concept of the independence of art commented on the role of art and culture in class society. It reflected the idea that art can only have a social role if it is free from the logic of domination. According to the Manifesto, only in this way could it contribute to a free society that shows an activist response towards exploitation and domination and where individuals can freely associate and determine themselves. This was a clear criticism of fascism and Stalinism, two dictatorships suffocating artistic expression as they were drowning workers' opposition, but it was also a comment on the role of art and culture in the social realm. The Manifesto was opposed then to the abstract idea that art could somehow be neutral in a class-based society.

The problem of the freedom of art, which has been the subject of critical analysis by academics as well as artists and philosophers such as Breton and Rivera (independent art), Schelling (infinity of art), and Hegelian-Marxist scholars such as Adorno and Marcuse (autonomy of art), concerns the question of the relationship of art and society. Exemplary of this is the relationship of art in wanting to intervene in other social systems such as politics, economy, culture, and others as many contemporary art curators and critics such as Maria Lind, Claire Bishop, Nicolas Bourriaud, Nicholas Serota, Michaela Crimmin, and Okwui Enwezor (to name just a few) have debated.

Some researchers and academics argue that certain social systems regulate the form and content of art. According to this approach, art is reduced to a certain part or state of society. As such, art might be considered as an automated echo of the state of the economy, or of the state of the political system. Lukács argues that reality exists objectively and independently of consciousness, and, therefore, apprehending the world would be a mere reflection of reality, without interpretation. In the same way, art would have to be a factual reflection of the totality of reality, providing an image of reality where the opposition between essence and appearance of reality appears united. According to this idea, artworks are closed universes that advance a more complete and livelier reflection of reality than the recipients – the citizens – have. For doing so, the role of art would not be to portray individual persons and situations, but representative characters under (general) representative social and cultural contexts. Art would then have to bear a rich account of life as it is in a whole, in its multiple experiences and, to do so, it would require a propaganda character (Lukács, 1954) that would aim at educating the masses, as in Stalinism (and other oppressing regimes such as Fascism).

Marx argues that fundamental changes in art can take place without fundamental changes in society, claiming for an autonomous art: "In the case of the arts, it is well known that certain periods of their flowering are out of all proportion to the general development of society" (Marx, 1859).

Traditional, objective theories of art such as the 18th century views of Baumgarten and Herder, present a different approach to the autonomy of art. These have seen art as the Ideal of Beauty. Perceiving Beauty as an endless value that is independent of changing human values, everyday life, human practice, and human interests, this idea presupposes then that art is intrinsically autonomous and aspiring for perfection. In these traditional art theories, art is seen as a system representing unlimited values that surpass society, being considered a system in a higher position in relation to other social systems (Fuchs and Holzner, 2005).

German sociologist Niklas Luhmann offers a more recent approach to looking at art as a social system. To Luhmann, who developed the idea of social systems theory, society is a social system with various subsystems and each one always holds a unique function in society. This means that one social system never does the same as another social system. According to this idea, art is a closed system and cannot work autonomously from other social systems to operate within the larger system of society. According to Luhmann, there would be no other system in society that does what art does which would be to offer a perception of reality as it is.

Whereas Breton and Rivera see the autonomy of art as crucial for its revolutionary role in society (1938), for Luhmann the question of autonomy is one of operational functions, not one that sees art as a specific system that has a role of looking critically at society; the evolution of art is fully determined by its own logic, there would be no external influences from other social systems or society. In his view, art is a social system that shows how reality is, not how it could be (1984).

While for Adorno the autonomy of art resides in the production of the work of art freed from external individual verdicts – "the autonomy of art lies in the work of art, in its production, not specifically in the aesthetic judgments of the subject" (1958) – for Luhmann the autonomy of art is a functional autonomy within society that is not different from the autonomy of the other subsystems of modern society (1984). The elements of social criticism are not central in Luhmann's theory of art. He thinks that it is due to their fictional character that works of art are able to criticise the shortcomings of society, but this possibility is not realised in every work of art. Hence, he continues, social criticism is not a constitutive feature in art and the function of art consists of its ability to arouse and maintain in us an awareness of the contingent nature of our phenomenal world (1990).

Whereas for Marcuse, the advantage of art lies in the reading or interpretation it gives of society by showing what it could be, more than portraying it in realistic terms (1978), for Luhmann, art would be inherently ambiguous. In this view, artworks would show clues on how to observe – on how to look at the world – but this would not be particularly relevant as observers are free to make their own interpretations. Different forms of art would be coherent in the way that all make observations that encourage other observations, putting the focus on the subjective realm of perception. Furthermore, in his systems' theory, Luhmann considers art is anything that is communicated as being art. Following this theory, the elements of the art system are not material artworks, but communications revolving around the ideas and meanings of art. If anything that presents itself as art is art, then art is a self-referential social system in the sense that any communication about art would always lead to more communications about art. The dynamic self-organisation of art would be based on observations that would allow other observations and on aesthetic codes based on the binomial beautiful/ugly, in a permanent construct and communication of definitions of beauty and ugliness (1984).

From Bourdieu's perspective, aesthetic codes are regarded differently. Bourdieu considers such codes to be the attitudes and dispositions of their social actors. On the level of their consciousness and self-understanding, social actors – in this case, certain art devotee groups – use aesthetic codes but, Bourdieu emphasised, sociology should not limit itself to the mere affirmation of this state of affairs; it should not limit itself to the phenomenology of aesthetic codes and attitudes. What it should do is to go beyond the individual actors' self-understanding and ask what consequences this kind of action has (Bourdieu, 1984; Bourdieu and Darbel, 1969).

In his production, Luhmann does not practise criticism in the same sense as critical theorists have practised it. Critical theorists have assumed that an adequate knowledge of societal reality is possible, and societal criticism therefore has a secure and truthful epistemological basis. Luhmann, on the other hand, thought that this kind of basis is not possible as, from this perspective, art is, on the one hand, based on second-degree observations and, on the other hand, in communication within its closed realm only.

The stories of the works of contemporary artists contradict Luhmann's self-referential definition of art as a social system. *A few howls again* (2010) by Silvia Kolbowski (b.1953, Argentina) is an exemplar of how art enters domains other than the artistic one. The video refers to the power of the media to create or mould stories which we then go on to accept unquestioningly as being true. The story of the death of Ulrike Meinhof (1934–1976), a founding member of the Red Army Faction (RAF; Rote Armee Fraktion), the German extreme left-wing group known for its acts of terrorism, is retold here from an alternative narrative that brings the past into the present in a reflection on global contemporary reality. There are many more examples, such as the body of work by Halil Altındere (b.1971, Turkey), who is one of several artists who have consistently explored political, social, and cultural codes to focus on the tools of resistance to oppressive systems. In *Wonderland* (2013), he presents the hip-hop group Tahribad-ı İsyan from the historic Sulukule neighbourhood in Istanbul. Inhabited by Roma communities since the Byzantine Empire, it is now subject to a process of urban development against the residents' wishes. In a snowball effect, the demonstrations against this gentrification process have multiplied in nationwide protests and strikes. In the video, imaginary scenes commonly associated with the marginalised life of this neighbourhood appear alongside the hip-hop group's activist voices.

Luhmann's idea of structural couplings (borrowed from Humberto Maturana) seems to point precisely to this relationship between different subsystems. Structural couplings designate that different systems may co-evolve over time and systematically communicate about the same themes and within specific contexts, but in their specific and different codes. This may be labelled co-evolution, interpenetration, or structural couplings (Luhmann, 1992). It may occur within and as part of organisations and projects, more or less formal institutions, or negotiating frameworks. Within the same organisational framework different systems and codes may learn to co-evolve and build common institutions despite the distinctive differences (Luhmann, 1992).

Structural couplings between art and other function systems, such as politics and economics, seem to be vital in the continuous production of artistic projects aiming for social change. In other words, as observed by Hal Foster, art alone cannot transform society. But – I would add – art, structurally coupled with other subsystems, in dual co-learning processes of differentiation and integration, might have the power to transform society.

Art as social practice

The term social practice runs like a silver thread through the writings of contemporary artists and art critics' meditations on art when defining an artwork that highlights encounter or asks for the participation of the audience. The literature referring to the term links it with ideas of participation, the possible role of art in society, and the combination of art with other disciplines, ideas that came across when analysing *Morrinho, Project Row Houses* and *Intervene: Heroes and Villains*.

From all the attempts to create a line of thought and put into words the possible meanings of social practice in realm of art in its relations with society, Nicolas Bourriaud's book *Esthétique Relationnelle* has come to be seen as a major text for a generation of artists and art critics who came to notoriety in Europe in the early to mid 1990s (Bishop, 2006) but also for researchers and students.

In this book, Bourriaud spoke of "the work of art as social interstice" (as cited in Bishop, 2006, p. 180). Consisting of a collection of essays, Bourriaud's book elevated a then new form of artistic production, putting the focus on artworks that took as their "theoretical horizon the realm of human interactions and its social context rather than the assertion of an independent and private symbolic space" (Bourriaud, 1998, p. 14). In this collection of essays, Bourriaud presented a framework for art practices of artists such as Rirkrit Tiravanija, Philippe Parreno, and Vanessa Beecroft who showed concerns with everyday life, human behaviour, and the production of convivial social spaces as well as the encouragement of "an inter-human intercourse which is different to the zones of communication that are forced upon us" (as cited in Bishop, 2006: 185). Bourriaud argued that relational art was a reinvestment in artistic practice as a means of learning to inhabit the world in a better way. To Bourriaud, relational art was an initiative to fight the outcomes of alienation and normalisation, which are characteristic to the modern and the contemporary worlds (Augé, 1995). According to this idea, relational art was also a tool to create temporary micro-utopias that would promote new models for democratic participation.

Bourriaud considers relational aesthetics to be a means of locating contemporary practice within the culture at large. Such understanding of relational art shifts a goods-based economy to a service-based one. It is also seen as a response to the virtual relationships of the Internet and globalisation, which on the one hand have prompted a desire for more physical and face-to-face interaction between people, while on the other hand have inspired artists to adopt a do-it-yourself practice and model their own "possible universes" (Bourriaud, 1998, p. 13). This emphasis on immediacy is mindful of 1960s performance art, which privileged the genuineness of a first-hand encounter between the audience and the artist's body.[1] To Bourriaud, the main difference between performance and relational art is the shift in attitude towards social change: instead of a "utopian" agenda, today's artists seek a micro-utopia as they only long to find provisional solutions in the here and now; instead of trying to change their environment, artists today are simply "learning to inhabit the world in a better way"; instead of looking forward to a future utopia, this art sets up functioning micro-utopias in the present (Bourriaud, 1998, p. 13). Bourriaud argues: "It seems more pressing to invent possible relations with our neighbours in the present than to bet on happier tomorrows" (Bourriaud, 1998, p. 45).

Two decades later, the discourse on relational, participatory, and socially engaged work, in artistic and curatorial practices has increased as demonstrated in artworks, art projects, exhibitions, and literature. Parallel to this, more terms were added to the discourse such as the educational turn in curatorial practices claimed by Paul O'Neill and Mick Wilson (2010) and Irit Rogoff (2008, 2010a, 2010b, 2013). This process of growth has been further strengthened by the recognition of art institutions and art universities. In 2008, stating that "originating with a desire to present a contemporary group exhibition that would capture the spirit of the art that emerged during the early 1990s (Guggenheim Museum, 2008)," the Guggenheim Museum in

New York organised a collective exhibition titled *theanyspacewhatever* joining artists "linked by a mutual rethinking of the early modernist impulse to conflate art and life. Rather than deploy representational strategies, they privilege experiential, situation-based work over discrete aesthetic objects (Guggenheim Museum, 2008)." Currently, there are dozens of college-level programmes promoting the study of art and social practice, in the United States of America (such as the M.F.A Social Practice Queens, Queens College, the Public Practice programme at Otis College of Art and Design, or The Moore College of Art and Design's M.F.A. in Community Practice); United Kingdom (such as the M.A. Art and Social Practice at Middlesex University or the M.A. with the same title at The University of the Highlands and Islands); and across Europe (such as the M.A. in Social Practice and the Creative Environment at the Limerick Institute of Technology).

Much of the exhibitions, the writings, and the academic programmes that have been created under the umbrella of social practice have attempted to find parallel historical roots between art and society, and many chose to place it in closer proximity to community arts and new-genre public art. Another way of looking at social practice has placed it together with the concept of social sculpture coined by Joseph Beuys in the 1970s and changes in activist practice brought on by the emergence of the anti-globalisation movement and the "Do-It-Yourself" ethos of the 1990s has the stories of the projects *Morrinho, Project Row Houses,* and *Intervene: Heroes and Villains,* presented in Chapter 3. The "Do-It-Yourself" philosophy, as it was termed in the early 1990s, has gained cultural traction, and has spread into the basic composition of urban living. Experiments in alternatives – from community gardens initiated by artists (as the group Urban Nomads, which organised workshops for gardening in the city, in Lisbon, 2011) to group meals in public space (as in the project *À Mesa/At the Table,* a project that brought people together for free shared meals in public space, by architect Luisa Alpalhão, in Lisbon, in 2012) and free advertising for local shops (as demonstrated by the project *Shop Local,* a project that consisted of the design of free, old-style advertising for small businesses on nearby building facades, by British artist Bob and Roberta Smith, in East London, in 2007) – have become a broad form of self-determined sociality and a common practice in the arts.

Marcellini and Rana have acknowledged that social practice has also been positioned "in the areas of spatial practice, artistic research, experimental geography, performance art, dance, and theatre" (2012). They argue "despite widespread contention over its origins, there is a growing consensus that the artistic field of social practice is defined by a focus on working with human subjects" (2012).

In the *Living as Form* (2011) exhibition catalogue, curator Maria Lind clarified that "unlike its avant-garde predecessors such as Russian Constructivism, Futurism, Situationism, Tropicalia, Happenings Fluxus, and Dadaism"; social practice is not an art movement but points to ways of life highlighting participation and challenging power relations and structures.

Furthermore, such practices span disciplines ranging from urban planning and community work to theatre and the visual arts (Lind, 2011). Lind argues that "Artists have long desired that art enters life" (2011) emphasising correlations between art, culture, and society or, in other words, between various social subsystems. In the same text, Lind connects art with the political. She clarifies this relationship through the example of works of artists ranging from passing a message, in an observational way as a means to shift perception to asking for participation which, in some cases, means taking real political action (2011).

According to curator Maria Lind "the interpersonal contains the seeds of political conflict inherently" (2011). In an interview for a publication conceived in the frame of the 2012 *There Is No Knife Without Roses* seminar at Tensta Konsthall, in Stockholm, on his project *Project Row Houses*, Rick Lowe stated "Everyone, no matter what occupation, or stage in life has creativity to offer to the process of socially engaged work" (Lowe, 2012).

A notable example of the relation of art and the social is the ongoing "do-it" series of exhibitions, seminars, and publications, which are divided in branches, as do-it (museum), do-it (home), do-it (TV), do-it (seminar), and an online do-it in collaboration with e-flux, among others. The scope of "do-it," initiated in 1993 and in 2013 presented as "do-it: the compendium" showed works of art embed in daily life and demanded participation in order to exist. Ai Weiwei instructed how to make a spray device to block a surveillance camera. Ben Kinmont asked the public to "invite a stranger into home for breakfast." Agnes Varda submitted a recipe for chard gratin, while Louise Bourgeois invited us to smile at a stranger and Yoko Ono encouraged people to keep wishing.

Alongside being a reference for contemporary art and the relationship between art and society today, in the last years, the term social practice and the relationship between art and society have been widely questioned in books, exhibitions, and symposiums by art historians, curators, and art critics such as Ina Blom, Maria Lind, Irit Rogoff, Claire Bishop, and Charles Esche. In her book *On the Style Site: Art, Sociality and Media Culture* (2007), Ina Blom examined works and practices of artists of the 1990s and argued for a new reading of the development of the idea of social practice in terms of the relationship between art and the question of style, in which the relations between appearance and social identity are negotiated (2007). Three years later, in 2010, a symposium at Tate Britain was entitled *Art and the Social: Exhibitions of Contemporary Art in the 1990s* and explored the social turn in exhibition-making in Europe and North America in the 1990s, looking at the part played by political activism, institutional critique, and forms of socialisation influenced by the media and the moving image. Questioning terms such as "Kontext Kunst," "social engagement," and "relational aesthetics," the participants discussed developments in recent contemporary exhibition history, including exhibitions staged outside of the art institution that engaged with site in the broadest sense. Claire Bishop, one of the guest speakers, discussed three exhibitions from 1993, *Culture in Action* in Chicago, *Unité d'Habitation* in Firminy, and *Sonsbeek* in Arnhem. Two years later, in 2012, Claire Bishop published *Artificial Hells: Participatory Art and the Politics of Spectatorship*, which critically examined important moments in the progress of a participatory aesthetic and the relation between art and the social claiming the "social turn" should be "positioned more accurately as a return to the social, part of an on-going history of attempts to rethink art collectively" (as cited in Larssen, 2012).

Middelburg Summer 1996 was an art project by Jens Haaning that showcased in the exhibition *Spectres of the Nineties* [2] and revealed, in a sharp way, a form of critique of the relations between art and the social. In this work, the artist relocated the entire production line of a small Turkish factory, including the workers (a dozen employees from Iran, Bosnia, and Turkey), the office, and the kitchen area and changing rooms into De Vleeshall, a Kunsthalle in the neighbouring seaside town of Middelburg, in The Netherlands.[3] While some authors have looked at this work as "socially committed contextual art" that arouses "questions concerning the correct handling of cultural import-export suddenly overlap with more concrete problems of migration" (Fricke, 2000), curator and academic Lars Bang Larssen argues that the work showed art and the social to be constantly swapping in context with each other and would never match (2012).

As Lars Bang Larssen noted, the social remains a recurring theme in artistic practice, art history, and as study programmes. It seems urgent to understand and locate the border of art's integration and relation with the social. Only then will it be possible to understand the true potential transforming power of art in society.

Art as social sculpture

Social sculpture is a term coined by German artist Joseph Beuys (1921–1986) through a series of public lectures in the early 1970s in America, under the title "Energy Plan for the Western Man." By social sculpture, Beuys meant a kind of artwork that would take place in the social realm, and, in order to be complete, would need social engagement and the participation of an audience (Kuoni, 1990). Beuys believed that as spectators became participants, the catalysis of social sculpture would lead to a transformation of society through the release of popular creativity:

> Only on condition of a radical widening of definition will it be possible for art and activities related to art to provide evidence that art is now the only evolutionary-revolutionary power. Only art is capable of dismantling the repressive effects of a senile social system to build a SOCIAL ORGANISM AS A WORK OF ART.
>
> (Beuys, 1973, as cited in Kuoni, 1990, p. 22)[4]

Beuys's approach demonstrates a concern with social change and not a concern with the transformation of art as something independent from society: "The position of freedom that he experiences at first hand – learns to determine the other positions in the TOTAL ARTWORK OF THE FUTURE SOCIAL ORDER" (Beuys, 1973, as cited in Bishop, 2006, p. 125).

With a passion for economics and politics, Beuys's art is inevitably aimed at social transformation. Beuys's 1983 lithograph *Creativity = Capital* illustrates a seeming chaos of arguments, designs, and proofs resonant of the artist's blackboard drawings in which he drew plans for his desired socially transformative art. Standing boldly on top of these plans, the headline Creativity = Capital overlaps the visual chaos in a way that turns it into a final and definite conclusion. This headline can be found in many of his other works and is often interpreted as an assertion for an expanded understanding of art in which creativity and capital are the fundamental forces for the reformation of society.

To Beuys, creativity was not exclusive to the arts' realm in the same way that capital was not the territory of corporations only. To him, both were equally present and available to all within their daily lives and practices. This idea implies that all areas of knowledge are available to all and that each one can intervene in the other. What became his popular motto "everyone is an artist," was perhaps deceptive, as it was not meant to ask everyone to produce art, as we know it. Rather, it was the logical refinement of his unique and sophisticated conception of human creativity as social sculpture, which to him was not a physical artwork but the result of the conscious actions of individuals and groups to reform their social, economic, and material conditions to free human creativity with a transforming, social aim rather than aspiring for a formal, artistic practice.

The aspect of Beuys's practice that still resonates for contemporary artists is based on the rhetoric of participation and democracy, so often linked to Bourriaud's relational aesthetics. The motivations for what came to be understood as the socially engaging quality of the work of Beuys and his fight for human emancipation were grounded in utopian desires rooted in the historical moment of post-World War II, which was marked by the collapse of revolutionary Marxism.

Beuys's notion of social sculpture and the overwhelming amount of dialogical and relational art being made today is part of a now long tradition of viewer participation and activated spectatorship in works of art across many media (Bishop, 2004), which implies observation and perception but always paired with an active and participatory attitude. A close consideration of the concept of relational art is intricate with Beuys's social sculpture as both a programme for art and a political vision for society. His concept influenced a panoply of art genres within contemporary art as participatory, socially engaged, and relational art today and provides a vehicle for understanding their histories as well as the relation between art and social change (Bishop, 2004).

Beuys's concept of social sculpture influenced, in fact, a wide variety of art genres within contemporary art and is a benchmark in the history of art in its relationship with the social realm (Bishop, 2004, p. 78) as its resonations in the overwhelming amount of dialogical and relational art being made today.

In Francesco Bonami's 2005 article for Tate Etc magazine, *The Legacy of a Myth Maker* coinciding with Tate Modern's exhibition *Joseph Beuys: Actions, Vitrines, Environments*, Bonami illustrates how contemporary artists have both borrowed and developed from Beuys's approach. In his text, Bonami exposes Thomas Hirschhorn (b.1957, Switzerland) as an example of one of the contemporary artists that take Beuys as a major source of influence: "Thomas Hirschhorn's work often has a social agenda with a political undertone." Bonami describes Hirschhorn's *Bataille Monument* at Documenta 11, in 2002, a collaborative project that gathered residents of a German suburb to build, install, and supervise a structure of eight provisional sheds including a TV studio, a snack bar, and a library with topography of Bataille's work. Bonami points to the emphasis of this work on social investigation through the participation of people who are not regular exhibition attendees. The difference between Hirschhorn and Beuys, Bonami explains, is the methodology: whereas Beuys preferred to use political tools, such as campaigning and protesting, Hirschhorn favoured artistic practices.

Other contemporary artists showing the influence of Beuys in their work choose political tools as their medium. This is the case of Hiwa K.'s (b.1975, Iraq) video *This Lemon Tastes of Apple* (2011), which documents the artist's participation on the last day before the two-month ban of protests against the Kurdish Regional Government that occurred in Iraq, Turkey, and Iran in 2011. As we watch the video, we see Hiwa K. in the midst of the crowd making the journey from Sarai Azadi (Liberty Square) to the border, while playing Ennio Morricone's *Once Upon a Time in the West* on a harmonica. With the sound amplified by a megaphone, the crowd hears the harmonica music, which is thereby given greater force and a magnified effect. The images depict the protesters wearing masks and holding lemons to protect themselves from the tear gas, in a reaction reminiscent of the 1988 Halabja Massacre. Since that time, the smell of tear gas – similar to the smell of apples – is associated with the country's political memory, notwithstanding all government attempts to erase it.

Many more examples could be given to illustrate the legacy of social sculpture and how participation became a transformative tool used in various ways by contemporary artists. As Hal Foster puts it in his book *Bad New Days: Art, Criticism, Emergency*, the avant-garde is not over, but perhaps more necessary today than it has ever been before. Foster clarifies that it's not in the sense of the heroic, historical avant-garde of "radical innovation" or "transgression," but an avant-garde that is "immanent in a caustic way," one that "seeks to trace fractures that already exist within a given order, to pressure them further, even to activate them somehow."[5]

Cultural studies in relation to social change

A lot of artistic projects aiming at social change seem to fail due to the lack of understanding and embedding the existent cultural references when trying to achieve social change – it is not that the projects deny the impact of culture on the process of social change but more that they seem to ignore how to integrate cultural references when aiming at social change. *Morrinho*, which will be described in Chapter 3, is particularly singular in terms of the empowerment the community gained through the project. It was initiated from within the community, implying the natural integration of existent cultural references and a full understanding of what change was, in fact, needed.

Defining culture

The term culture has been used in various senses. In the field of economics Cremer and Gahvari (1993), following Arrow (1974), defines culture as that portion of a stock of knowledge that is shared by a substantial segment of a group, but not by the general population from which that group is drawn (Cremer and Gahvari. 1993); Arrow, 1974). Outside of economics, definitions of culture vary much more widely. According to UNESCO, culture encompasses art and literature, lifestyles, ways of living together, value systems, traditions, and beliefs (UNESCO, 1982, 2001). Kroeber and Kluckhohn defined culture as the set of "patterns, explicit and implicit, of and for behaviour acquired and transmitted by symbols, constituting the distinctive achievement of human groups, including their embodiment in artefacts". At the heart of this idea of culture are the traditional (such as historically derived and selected) ideas and especially their linked values. Furthermore, it considered culture system both as products of action and as conditioning elements of further action (Kroeber and Kluckhohn, 1952).

An observation of the history of cultural studies shows that the diversity of the discipline currently proliferating is vast. For the aims of this study the historical movements identified and chosen are the University of Birmingham Centre for Contemporary Cultural Studies and the Frankfurt School.

Both movements focused on the intersections of culture and ideology and regarded ideology critique as crucial to critical cultural studies (Centre for Contemporary Cultural Studies, 1980a, 1980b). Both saw culture as a mode of ideological reproduction and hegemony, in which cultural forms may have a role in shaping the ways of thought and behaviour that stimulate individuals to adapt to the social conditions of capitalist societies. Both also looked at culture as a potential form of resistance to capitalist society, as well as a mode of social reproduction, and both the earlier forerunners of British cultural studies, especially Raymond Williams (1958 and 1961), and the theorists of the Frankfurt school, conceived of high culture as forces of resistance to capitalist modernity (Williams, 1958 and 1961).

Both traditions thus deployed theory as a mode of conceptualising the general contours of the established mode of historical development and analysed the conjunctions of culture and society in relation to certain historical contexts. Horkheimer and Adorno's concept of the culture industry might be seen broadly as a philosophical analysis of the configuration of society and culture that emerged in the era of state and monopoly capitalism in the 1930s and 1940s in Europe and the United States; the analyses of the decline of working class culture, the rise of a commercialised mass culture, and emergence of new oppositional cultures within British cultural studies can likewise be seen as a form of broad theoretical discourse often associated with philosophy or a philosophically-mediated social theory (Hall et al., 1980).

From the beginning, British cultural studies was highly political in nature and focused on the potentials for resistance in oppositional subcultures, first, valorising the potential of working class cultures, then, youth subcultures to resist the hegemonic forms of capitalist domination. Unlike the classical Frankfurt School (but similar to Herbert Marcuse), British cultural studies turned to youth cultures as providing potentially new forms of opposition and social change. Through studies of youth subcultures, British cultural studies demonstrated how culture came to constitute distinct forms of identity and group membership and appraised the oppositional potential of various youth subcultures (Hall and Jefferson, 1976). Cultural studies came to focus on how subcultural groups resist dominant forms of culture and identity, creating their own style and identities. With a postmodern turn in cultural studies, there was an increasing emphasis on the audience and how audiences produce meanings and how cultural texts produce both popular pleasures and forms of resistance (Fiske, 1989a, 1989b).

Scott Lash argues that cultural studies is entering a new phase. He put forth an idea that lays the focus on power as a generative force. According to Lash, "Hegemony was the concept that de facto crystallised cultural studies as a discipline." Hegemony usually refers to the "preponderant influence or domination of one nation over another" (Griffin, 2012). To him, the flow of power is becoming more internalised, and there has been "a shift in power from the hegemonic mode of power over to an intensive notion of power from within (including domination from within) and power as a generative force" (Lash, 2007). Instead of the power of one towards the other, this shift puts the power of one in oneself.

In the past decade, cultural critics of all sorts have advanced different concepts to address the widespread emergence of initiatives that – through art and creativity – have approached society's most pressing issues, from the use of power to massive human rights abuses, from globalisation to social injustice (Sommer, 2006; Yúdice, 2003). And in the wake of the so-called Third Wave of democratisation, Latin American cities as diverse as Bogotá, Buenos Aires, Lima, Mexico City, and Rio de Janeiro have become the privileged loci of cultivation for these kind of initiatives.

In his article *Culture and Social Movements*, Doug McAdam argued that there is a significant "rationalist" and "structural" bias in the studies of social movements that deny the impact of culture on the process of social change. Until recently, he argues, "culture in all of its manifestations, was rarely invoked by American scholars as a force in the emergence and development of social movements" (McAdam, 1994).

While scholars like McAdam insist that cultural forces have been ignored in the process of studying social movements, others insist that cultural strategies are the primary means of social change for an era of new social movements that began to emerge out of the 1960s. With the emergence of "new social movements," Alberto Melucci argues that constitutive cultural strategies are the primary and the most important acts of contemporary social movements. Conflicts of new social movements do not chiefly express themselves through action designed to achieve outcomes in the political system. Rather, they raise a challenge that recasts the language and cultural codes that organise information. The ceaseless flow of messages only acquires meaning through the codes that order the flux and allow its meaning to be read and integrated. The forms of power now emerging in contemporary societies are grounded in an ability to "inform," that is, to "give form" (Melucci, 1980).

The idea of integrating existing cultural references in projects for social change has been studied in several programmes and respective toolkits, in particular when looking at communities that are characterised by diversity in terms of culture. In 2011, UNESCO published "The Cultural Diversity Lens: A practical tool to integrate culture in development – Pedagogical Guide." The lens toolkit contains a general introduction on the cultural diversity–programming lens, a step-by-step guide on how to use and develop a lens, draft general framework, and four thematic lenses. It further includes a copy of the Universal Declaration on Cultural Diversity, an introduction to indicators, and the key terms and definitions. In this publication/toolkit, it was argued that integrating existing cultural references was needed for success in projects: "Dialogue with the populations concerned, taking their culture into account and respecting their human rights – particularly their cultural rights – are essential to the success of all projects, programmes or policies" (UNESCO, 2011). It also argued for respect of the existent cultural references: "Understanding, appreciating and respecting the cultures of the populations concerned (language, religion, history, lifestyle, decision-making bodies, communication methods, social structure) is essential for everyone's access and involvement" (UNESCO, 2011, p. 9). As an example, the text points to the framework of an education policy: "the use of pedagogical content in a language different from the one of the populations concerned constitutes an obstacle to their access to the content" (UNESCO, 2011, p. 9).

Furthermore, the text argues that embedding local knowledge in projects is a key factor for success: "Intangible heritage such as local knowledge and knowhow can prove to be a key factor for programme success in areas such as education, health, managing natural resources or agriculture" (UNESCO, 2011, p. 10).

In the same year, the toolkit "Guidance for Integrating Culturally Diverse Communities into Planning for and Responding to Emergencies: A Toolkit" was developed to "provide preparedness planning and response agencies, organisations, and professionals with practical strategies, resources and examples of models for improving existing activities and developing new programs to meet the needs of racially and ethnically diverse populations" (Andrulis, Siddiqui, and Purtle, 2011). This toolkit referred to the need not only for identification but also for understanding culture within specific and varied communities: "An important first step is to identify and understand the distinctive needs of diverse communities, particularly as they relate to race, ethnicity, culture, language and trust" (Andrulis, Siddiqui, and Purtle, 2011). In the toolkit, it is argued that only through experience is it possible to fill in the gaps of strategies for grasping communities.

Besides the more practical approaches towards the integration of existing cultural references in projects for social change, the term integration has also been studied in various theoretical approaches. Paul Hoffmann, the director for the Marshall Plan[6], used for the first time the term integration to describe the process whereby states transfer their sovereignties to a supranational centre. Scholars have also defined integration in terms of international order and structures of governance. Karl Deutsch back in 1957 defined integration as the creation of peace zones and "the attainment, within a territory, of a sense of community" and of institutions and practices strong enough and widespread enough to assure, for a "long time, dependable expectations of peaceful change among its population" (Deutsch et al., 1957).

Another theorist of integration, Ernst B. Haas, defined integration as a process "whereby political actors in several distinct national settings are persuaded to shift their loyalties, expectations and political activities toward a new centre, whose institutions possess or demand jurisdiction over the pre-existing national states" (Haas, 1958). According to Haas, integration is "the voluntary creation of larger political units involving the self-conscious eschewal of force in relations between participating institutions" (as cited in Lindberg and Scheingold, 1971). Harrison referred to the role of institutions in the process of integration and therefore defined integration as "the attainment within an area of the bonds of political community, of central institutions with binding decision-making powers and methods of control determining the allocation of values at the regional level" (Harrison, 1974).

In European studies, scholars such as Castells and Melucci raised awareness of the need of association of European integration with culture as a matter of respect towards the diversity of European cultures. "European integration lacks a cultural dimension comparable to that of nation states" (Delanty, 2000). Castoriadis argues that the cultural dimension is as important as the economic one for understanding and transforming society (Castoriadis, 1987). This dimension expands to questions of identity (Garcia, 1993; Schleslinger, 1994; Smith, 1995; Wintle, 1996). For Soysal, "much of the debate on European integration and identity privileges the legitimate 'actor hood' of nation-states or intergovernmental negotiation and decision-making structures" (Soysal, 2002).

All these studies point towards the importance of understanding and integration when different cultural references come into play. As obvious as this conclusion may sound it is still a challenge faced by artistic projects for social change and it is important to reflect on why this is a recurrent problem implying the failure of such (mostly good intentioned) projects.

Discourses of multidisciplinarity in cultural studies

Crossing borders of disciplines is usually linked to a tendency to push the boundaries of class, gender, race, sexuality, and the other elements that differentiate individuals from each other and through which people build their identities. Therefore, most forms of cultural studies, and most critical social theories, have engaged various multicultural theories, which focus on exemplifications of gender, race, ethnicity, and sexuality resulting in the critical discourses that have emerged since the 1960s. Multidisciplinarity in cultural studies[7] consequently seems to draw on a contrasting range of discourses and fields to theorise the complexity and contradictions of the multiple effects of a vast range of cultural forms in human lives and also demonstrates how these forces serve not only as instruments of domination, but also as means for confrontation and change.

The main traditions of cultural studies combine social theory, cultural critique, history, philosophical analysis, and specific political interventions, thus overcoming the standard idea of specialisation or single-disciplinary approaches. Cultural studies thus appears to operate within a multidisciplinarity conception that draws on social theory, economics, politics, history, communication studies, literary and cultural theory, philosophy, and other theoretical disciplines. This is an approach shared by the Frankfurt School and British cultural studies. Multidisciplinary approaches to culture and society transgress borders between various academic disciplines.[8]

Such multidisciplinarity approaches suggest that one should not stop at the border of an observation but should see how various observations are subject to participative construction and articulated in discourses in a given socio-historical conjuncture. Multidisciplinary approaches thus involve border crossings across disciplines from observation to context of a culture and a social reality (Williams, 1958, 1961).

Since the 1970s, the research agenda for the humanities and social sciences as well as conventional disciplines has taken up cultural questions within their own specific areas of activity. Disciplines such as history, fine arts, sociology, human geography, international relations, English, education, architecture, psychology, philosophy, economics, and politics have undergone a so-called "cultural turn." This happened while anthropology, which is traditionally the discipline regarded as the one owning culture as its object of study, has been meticulously influenced by cultural studies hypothesising. Cultural analysis is today an enormously common and distributed intellectual venture, so much so, as Johnson et al. have perceived, that cultural studies itself is currently "no longer in a pioneering situation" when discussing cultural analysis (Johnson et al, 2004).

Despite cultural studies being regarded as intrinsically somehow beyond the disciplines, there is a lot of vagueness in this kind of description. As a broad creation, cultural studies, more or less multidisciplinary in its origins, has over time institutionalised itself as a discipline in itself, complete with its own historical roots, recognised texts, peculiar modes of questioning and arguing, styles of writing, and distinct object and expression of value preferences (popular instead of high culture; hybridity instead of purity; heterogeneity instead of homogeneity; the marginal instead of the mainstream; the new instead of the old). Besides this, cultural studies is present in journals, conferences, and professional associations as most classical disciplines. From this perspective, cultural studies is a discipline but also a facilitator of dialogue and exchange with people who work within other disciplinary contexts, showing an openness to what the other disciplines might consider the blind spots of cultural studies.

As Warner has remarked, disciplines "allow people to speak in code and forget questions that might be posed from the outside" (Warner, 2003, p. 116). It is the opening up to such questions from the outside – and taking them seriously enough to look for answers – that enables innovation and renewal in cultural studies, preventing it from closing in within its own consolidated boundaries. For example, in a reflection on the interface of political theory and cultural studies, professor of political science Jodi Dean, has argued that a conversation between these two distinct disciplinary fields is especially useful for thinking about politics at a time when the political and the cultural are so inextricably intertwined: "To put it bluntly, political theory risks oversimplifying its accounts when it fails to acknowledge the multiplicity of political domains. Cultural studies risks non-intervention by presuming its political purchase in advance" (Dean, 2000).

Opening cultural studies up to interventions from outside its own discursive field might imply building on the competencies, achievements, and aspirations of cultural studies but taking it into a more concretely social and practical direction, in a genuinely collaborative multidisciplinary approach, besides the selective borrowings from writings in other disciplines. As Marjorie Garber argues in her book *Academic Instincts*, "a really intensive encounter of two or more disciplines", involving the "need to learn each other's mental moves, rhetoric, and styles of thought, taking nothing for granted" (Garber, 2001, p. 74) is an exciting and needed endeavour. How to make it a fruitful one in which a transformation of society occurs remains a contested field.

A brief introduction to the history of classical project management in the cultural sector

Many projects for social change initiated by artists within artistic institutions and NGOs and the development sector fail despite the good intentions. It seems that, among other things, these projects lack good and rigorous planning and strategy. The analysis of Morrinho as well as the study of the links between creative and scientific disciplines presented in the subsequent chapters show an alternative narrative to project management providing an alternative perspective to this discipline in contrast to the mainstream or, in other words, to its grand narrative. To understand what this alternative might be, it may be interesting to make a quest for a commented reading list on this grand narrative.

Many artistic projects such as *Morrinho, Project Row Houses* or *Intervene: Heroes and Villains*, further described in Chapter 3, seem to acknowledge the discipline of project management but, apparently, without fully understanding or applying its rules and procedures.

There are many approaches towards classical project management and its history. Nevertheless, for this research, which addresses artistic projects created either within artistic institutions, NGOs, or non-profit humanitarian organisations in the development sector, the focus is on the debate of project management amongst humanitarian and cultural players. This is a long unsolved issue over which no overall consensus has been reached giving rise to various interpretations inscribed into different value systems. While it is widely recognised that good intentions are no longer sufficient in an aid world of increasing professionalism and accountability, the question often raised is what kind of quality is required in humanitarian and cultural aid players from whom and for what.

The Project Management Institute (PMI) acknowledges that project management "has always been practiced informally, but began to emerge as a distinct profession in the mid-20th century" (Project Management Institute, 2013). Even though project management is claimed to be a methodological discipline employed by NGOs, UN agencies, and non-profit organisations – including in the artistic and cultural sectors – to carry out and manage their projects and programmes, its practice in these sectors is still carried out at informal and not fully professional or informed levels. It is common to see artistic and cultural organisations hiring project managers with a background in art history or curating with experience in arts management. But does a project hold the same meaning in the arts, in the humanitarian, and in the managerial domains? Is an artistic project within the social and humanitarian domain managed – or should it be managed – in the same ways?

To answer these questions, it might be useful to look at project management's definitions of project and management. According to the Project Management Institute, a project is "a temporary group activity designed to produce a unique product, service or result." Furthermore, "a project is temporary in that it has a defined beginning and end in time, and therefore defined scope and resources." The Institute gives examples of what a project might be – "The development of software for an improved business process, the construction of a building or bridge, the relief effort after a natural disaster, the expansion of sales into a new geographic market – all are projects."

Moreover, "all must be expertly managed to deliver the on-time, on-budget results, learning and integration that organisations need" (PMI, 2013).

When looking for the definition of management under the lenses of project management, the most repeated statement seems to be "management is what managers do" which suggests the difficulty of defining management, the shifting nature of definitions, as well as the connection of managerial practices with the existence of a managerial cadre or class.

Historically, the practice of modern management owes its origin to the 16th century enquiry into low efficiency and failures of certain enterprises, conducted by the English statesman Sir Thomas More (1478–1535; Ratra, 2009, p. 2). Henri Fayol defined management in six administrative functions: forecasting, planning, organising, commanding, coordinating, and controlling (Fayol, 1916). American writer, social worker, political theorist, and organisational consultant, Mary Parker Follett described management as a philosophy, defining it as "the art of getting things done through people" (as cited by Barrett, 2003, p. 51).

As for project management as a discipline, according to Wæver, it "describes the tools, techniques, processes and structures suited to accomplishing the objectives of a defined project." Furthermore, Wæver situates the use of project management as a discipline in the 1960s only and identifies the first book with project management in its title (*Project Management* by John Stanley Baumgartner, published by R.D. Erwin in 1963; Wæver, 2007, p. 14).

Moving on to the uses of project management in the humanitarian field (in which artistic and cultural projects aim to operate), it is important to recognise the creation of the Project Management for Non Governmental Organisations (PM4NGOs) in 2010 as a new international NGO, in Washington, DC, USA. PM4NGOs was born precisely from the acknowledgement of the importance of and need for the use of professional project management methods in the development sector (PM4NGOs, 2013).

With a pedagogical purpose, the organisation created a series of learning guides such as "The Introduction of Project Management for Development Professionals – PMDPro, 2013." Under the theme "Changing the world through projects," the guide explains that development organisations manage their work through projects but the professional application of project management is usually overlooked: "Organisations tend to hire programmatic specialists (agronomists, public health professionals, economists, etc.), who are then asked to manage projects and lead project teams" (PM4NGOs, 2013). In this Guide's Introduction, it is argued "it is not as common, however, to find that they have extensive experience and skills in the area of project management" (PM4NGOs, 2013). Similarly, in the artistic and cultural field, is not unusual to find a good architect or art historian being promoted to project manager just for her or his technical or academic competence. While it is true that one must have a good understanding of the technical and conceptual aspects of the project, the principal areas of competence that are required in the management competence areas include technical; leadership/

interpersonal; personal/self-management; development/sector specific (PM4NGOs, 2013). These skills have been identified as often disregarded when appointing a project manager and are often inserted within functional support provided by the organisations' operations departments, such as accounting, human resources, and logistics (Diaz-Albertini, 1993).

Directed at project managers and team members who are new to project management, the 2013 guide by PM4NGOs raises questions, regarding the informal use of project management:

> Are project estimates accurate? Have project risks been anticipated and are they thoroughly controlled? Are project plans comprehensive and detailed? Is project progress monitored at all levels? Are project challenges identified, tracked and addressed? And, are all aspects of the project proactively managed throughout the life of the project? Are the social changes the project wishes to address being achieved?
>
> (PM4NGOs, 2013, p. 1)

These questions end in a series of five principles for the use of project management in the development sector (Figure 1.1): 1. Balance (all phases in the life of a project should be taken rigorously); 2. Comprehension (project management rules should be applied to manage consistently all the work through all phases of the life of a project); 3. Integration (all aspects of project management should be coordinated to ensure all elements of project design, planning, monitoring, and implementation run smoothly); 4.

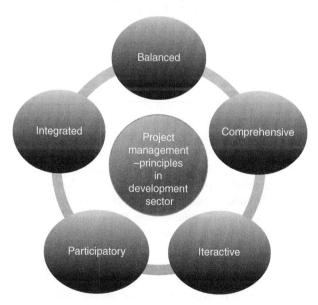

Figure 1.1 Five principles of project management in the development sector (adapted from PM4NGOs, 2013)

Participation (various stakeholders should be involved in the identification, design, planning, implementation, and monitoring of the project to ensure transparency, improve quality, increase human capacity and resources, and give strength to buy-in at all levels); and 5. Iterative (revisit and repeat project management processes in the life of a project in order to make sure that the project designs, project plans, and intended results are the same as initially).

Besides setting principles, PMD Pro Guide also pointed to challenges in the management of projects in the development sector which were presented as similar to the management of projects in other sectors including:

1 Delivering project results in the context of time, budget, quality, scope, risk, and benefit constraints;
2 Developing comprehensive and detailed project plans and managing them through the entire life of the project;
3 Managing projects that are often implemented via contractors, sub-contractors, and suppliers; and
4 Identifying potential risks and establishing processes to avoid and address these risks and ensuring that the intended project benefits are delivered (p. 7).

Furthermore, Nguyen, Sherif, and Newby (2007) identify obstacles for successful project implementations and accomplishments in developing countries mostly in terms of slow adaptation to project management techniques, political and social systems, cultural differences, and lack of financial support.

John Cropper, one of the founders of PM4NGOs, clarifies that "the problem of not applying professionally PM is very common and many NGOs don't really get PM – which is why scope drifts and projects are often overspent and/or late" (J. Cropper, personal communication, June 3, 2013). Poor project performance might be described as lack of effective project management training for project managers (Nguyen, Sherif, and Newby, 2007, p. 102) which is simply non-existent in informal applications of project management.

Another severe obstacle for successful project management systems implementation in developing countries as well as in NGOs and non-profit organisations is lack of senior management support due to fear of losing their control over projects, and their concept of inapplicability of the project management methodology, that is related to transparency and accountability aspects of managing projects. Besides, the following areas appeared to be important obstacles: lack of teamwork, ineffective management of subcontractors, rigid vertical organisation structures (Nguyen, Sherif, and Newby, 2007, p. 103). Most of the obstacles identified have their origin in organisational culture.

The methodology implementation of project management is strongly affected by organisational culture (Mochal and Mochal, 2003) and the project manager should take into account the culture of different organisations and even subcultures of the departments involved in the project (Elmes and Wilemon, 1988). In this relationship between project management and organisational culture, Harold Kerzner insists: "project management is a culture, not policies and procedures" (2004, p. 366).

Going back to the questions "does a project hold the same meaning in the arts, in the humanitarian, and in the managerial domains? Is an artistic project within the social and humanitarian domain managed – or should it be managed – in the same ways?" the guide "The Introduction of the Project Management for Development Professionals – PMDPro, 2013" answers that "a project Manager's job should NOT be reduced to a set of rigid rules that are applied thoughtlessly across each and every project, programme or portfolio." Additionally, it states "Project Management is as much 'art' as 'science'. There will be circumstances where a PM tool or technique could be used but, for any number or good reasons, might NOT be the smartest choice" (p. 129).

Dealing with complexity in social change: cross-cultural complex project management

As Louis Klein has stated, "we have become accustomed to quantifying the success rate of projects, at an average of 30 percent. Conversely, we expect up to 70 percent of all projects to fail" (Klein, 2012). One common problem found in projects for social change is that NGOs and non-profit organisations in the development sector tend to design large and complex projects. In fact, projects for social change aim to address complex problems of poverty, inequality, and injustice and, therefore, tend to operate in exceptionally challenging contexts (limited resources, high risks, complex procurement networks, unstable political/financial environments, unsafe conditions; PM4NGOs, 2013). Art-based projects for social change are projects within the humanitarian field and they seem to be on less sure ground whenever aims and strategy are not clear, when different aids, opinions, and thoughts come together, and, especially, if cultural differences come into play.

A focus on culture and complex project management has been seen as a possibility for stepping out of the single-disciplinary discourses and, subsequently, creating social change through projects. According to Louis Klein, "innovation in project management means leaving the well-known engineering framework and orienting oneself towards disciplines, sciences and professions, which offer alternatives for understanding and negotiation" (Klein, 2012).

Before addressing the idea of complexity in projects, it is important to look at the possible meaning of complexity in a wider domain. Not surprisingly, complexity has been defined in various ways, theories, and disciplines. Luhmann discussed the issue of complexity in many of his works, giving it a coherent methodological improvement with his theory of autopoietic systems, operationally closed, and differentiated. He starts with a conception of complexity related to its object of analysis – the world – such as the totality of all the events (in the world), and leads on to an epistemic methodological conception elaborated and better developed in his theoretical texts, when he begins to accept complexity as a concept of observation and description, that is, counting on the necessary presence of an observer who observes the complexity: the second order observer which concerns the observation of observations, that is, to identify the differentiations the systems make to observe. In this sense, the second order observer does not observe facts, but how the systems operate to access the facts of the environment in accordance with its structure (Luhmann, 1995).

Luhmann, in his social theory, imagines the world[9] as the highest unit of reference. In this view, the world is not a system because it does not have an environment from which he could be delimited. It also cannot be seen as an environment, since each environment presupposes an interior that, in turn, does not belong to the environment. Thus, the world is neither a system nor an environment, but it encompasses all the systems and their respective environments; it is the system/environment unit. According to this perspective, changing situations, maintenance of systems, systems' disappearance, all of it occurs in the world. This is why Luhmann as the ultimate reference chose the world as a category. The world cannot be surpassed; it does not have boundaries through which an environment extends, to which it could expand (Luhmann, 1993).

In this context, complexity means the totality of possible events and circumstances: something is complex if it involves, at least, more than one circumstance (as different cultures, different aims, and different disciplines). Increasing the number of possibilities, the number of relations between the elements grows in proportion and so does the complexity. The concept of world complexity represents the last boundary, or the ultimate last limit. If it is possible, it is possible only in the world.

This ultimate complexity of the world, in this form, cannot be understood by the human conscience. The human capacity cannot apprehend the complexity, considering all possible events and all the circumstances in the world. Thus, between the ultimate complexity of the world and the human conscience there is a gap. And it is there that the social systems play their role. They take on the task of reducing complexity. Social systems, to Luhmann (1995), interfere with the ultimate complexity of the world and man's limited ability to work the complexity.

In this context, the complexity theory (also known as Chaos Theory) in its study of nonlinear dynamic systems, promises to be a useful conceptual framework that reconciles the essential unpredictability of industries with the emergence of distinctive patterns (Cartwright, 1991). Although the theory was originally developed in the context of physical and biological sciences, Butler (1990), Kiel and Elliott (1996), and Radzicki (1990), among others, have noted that social, ecological, and economic systems also tend to be characterised by nonlinear relationships and complex interactions that evolve dynamically over time. This recognition has led to a surge of interest in applying complexity theory to a number of fields, including medicine (Goldberger, Rigney, and West, 1990), international relations (Mayer-Kress and Grossman,

1989), and economics (Baumol and Benhabib, 1989; Kelsey, 1988). Some authors appear overcome with great zeal in their enthusiasm for chaos, raising mystical and biblical associations. Merry's viewpoint might bring some light to the understanding of chaos in our lives: "deep chaos is a natural, inescapable essential stage in the transformation of all life forms. Out of chaos come forth the fertile variety of forms of existence and life in this universe" (Merry, 1995).

It has been argued that projects in general should be understood as a complex, dynamic system (Bertelsen, 2002), for instance when speaking of projects in developing countries and NGOs and in terms of the cultural differences within the communities as well as between stakeholders and within the organisation. The exploration of complexity within this research considers that all projects are complex to some extent and focuses merely on a specific source for this complexity, the cultural one.

Against this backdrop, it might be important to clarify the different terminologies multi-, inter-, and cross-cultural. At an individual level, just as a lot of people speak more than one language, many share more than one culture and respective codes with different groups of people interacted with. This suggests mixing or multiplicity, and the ability to function in at least two different groups. At a society level, the term multicultural does not essentially mean that each individual belongs to many different cultures (Fries, n/d). Multiculturalism implies that a variety of cultures is allowed to co-exist, if not form the sine qua non of what it means to exist as a human being (Kanpol and McLaren, 1995).

On the other hand, the term "intercultural" implies interaction. The term intercultural communication refers to communication between people from different cultures (Ting-Toomey, 1999) and "also refers to symbolic exchange processes whereby individuals from two or more different cultural communities negotiate shared meaning in an interactive situation" (Ting-Toomey, 1999).

Klineberg (1964) points out that "we find that culture differs widely from one another in the amount of emotional expression which is permitted. We speak for example of the imperturbability of the American Indian, the inscrutability of the oriental" (p. 174). Thus, it might be argued that the ways people communicate, their language as well as their nonverbal manners, all are determined by culture (Klopf and Park, 1982). In the educational field, cross-cultural applies to something which covers more than one culture. According to Fries (n/d), "a cross-cultural study of education in Western Europe would be a comparison of chosen aspects of education in various countries or regions, but would consider each country or region separately and would not suggest any interaction between the various educational systems" (p. 6).

Whereas multicultural implies a variety of cultures co-existing, intercultural suggests interaction, and in cross-cultural, each culture is compared to another but considered separately. Cross-cultural refers to the idea of integrating, embedding, and respecting the existent cultures of a community as the case of *Morrinho*, further described in Chapter 3, exemplifies.

Geert Hofstede and Fons Trompenaars conducted leading studies of cross-cultural management. Both approaches proposed a set of cultural dimensions along which dominant value systems could be ordered. These value systems would affect human thinking, feeling, and acting, and the behaviour of organisations and institutions in predictable ways. The two sets of dimensions reflect basic problems that any society has to cope with but for which solutions differ. Hofstede's study of the cultural dimensions, conducted in the 1970s and first published in 1980, mapped over 50 countries on a limited number of cultural dimensions. Some researchers have regarded Hofstede's study as landmark 30 years ago yet today less plausible and more criticised (e.g., McSweeney, 2002; Hofstede, 2003, 2005; Javidan et al., 2006), because of the changing pattern of socialisation and increased hybridisation of cultural contents due to intensive communications on a global scale, with the so-called Internet effect.

While all projects operate in a specific culture (or cultures) implying complexity to some degree, complexity management works on different levels, in a structured crescendo way: Complexity management focuses on four levels:

> When I think about leadership and management, I always start with myself, leading myself. The second point brings the others into view: leading others – how do I lead others? Third, leading organisations, the ability to read the organisation as a social system, the ability to read their policy and culture and to assess their options, is still widely neglected today. And as the fourth point, leading change.
>
> (Klein, 2011/2012, p. 15).

"Leading change" suggests here various levels. The research looked into the idea of change management because when critically analysing projects for social change, it was important to understand the various levels and dimensions of change within the organisational. Organisational change and its management have in fact become a huge field of study and practice. Several schools of thought contribute to an improved understanding of the complex phenomena of change (c.f., e.g., Pettigrew, Woodman and Cameron, 2001; Ven de Van and Poole, 1995). Change has been defined as a departure of the organisation from the status quo (Huber and Glick, 1993) or as a difference in the form, quality, or state of the organisation's alignment with the environment over time (Ven de Van and Poole, 1995).

Ven de Van and Poole (1995) made an ambitious attempt to develop an all-encompassing theoretical framework for interpreting change process theories throughout every conceivable kind of human organisational set-up in the field of social sciences. Whetten (2005) showed views of organisations as things or social actors and argued "organisational scholars should be experts on organisations, a peculiar type of social entity, and organisational settings, a peculiar type of social context" (p. 13). Following Heath and Sitkin (2001), Whetten called upon scholars to study uniquely organisational subjects – those "Big-O concepts," such as the identity, structure, culture, and performance that were seen as central to successful organisational enterprise. The author argued that organisations should be studied as nouns (social entities), rather than as verbs (social processes).

Broadly speaking, organisational change has been categorised as possessing three distinct but inter-related dimensions – context, content, and process (Pettigrew, 1985). The context is the situation surrounding the organisation. Pettigrew (1985) characterises the context as being either outer or inner to the organisation. Outer context refers to the political, economic, social, techno-logical, regulator, and competitive environment where the organisation operates. The inner context refers to the internal environment of the organisation – its corporate culture, structure, formal and informal processes, political context, and power centres. In these terms, context may be seen as referring to the "why" of change (Pettigrew, 1985).

Similarly, the content and process dimensions of change distinguish between the "what" of change as opposed to the "how" of change (Pettigrew, 1985). Thus, change as content or nouns (social entities; Whetten, 2005) looks at organisational parameters before and after an event in the life of the organisation – change – and tries to understand what the possible antecedents and consequences of the change could have been (Huber and Glick, 1993). In contrast to change as content or nouns, change as process is concerned with understanding the actual change as it unfolds, including the role of the man-ager as change agent. The process school is thus focused on studying change as a phenomenon that transforms the organisation (Pettigrew, 1990). Carroll and Hannan (2004) summed these differences:

> Content change refers to what actually differs in the organisation at the two points in time ... [whereas] process change ... [is] the way the change in content occurs – the speed, sequence of activities, decision-making and communication systems deployed, and the resistance encountered.
>
> (p. 358)

Allison (2002) reviewed the number of books concerned with non-profit management carried by Amazon.com and estimated that only about 10 per cent were concerned with non-profit leadership – virtually all of which were based on the US experience and were concerned with board and governance issues. Much of the current leadership research is therefore not relevant to the complex social, cross-cultural, and political environments in which NGO leaders work and manage (Hailey and James, 2004). The INTRAC Praxis programme tried to address this gap through the Praxis Papers and Notes.

In *The PraxisNote N°1 - How Can Knowledge Transferability Be Managed Across Cultures?* (Jackson and Sorgenfrei, 2003), where the idea of cross-cul-tural in NGOs was explored, it was argued that even though the core business of development NGOs involves working across cultures, the literature about NGO management hardly mentions the idea of culture and cross-cultural:

The recent 'discovery' of cross-cultural management theorists, particularly of Geert Hofstede (1980), by the academic development community in general (e.g. Dia, 1996) and those addressing NGO management in particular (e.g. Lewis, 2001) has not served to tackle many issues, only to highlight some of the problems. For example, such theory rarely considers issues of cross-cultural dynamics, including power relations, and processes by which hybrid forms of organisation develop.

(Jackson and Sorgenfrei, 2003).

Lewis goes further and considers that development work frequently involves a cross-cultural encounter of some sort between the community and foreigners and, because of that, cultural sensitivity between NGO staff and local communities is a relevant management issue (Lewis, 2003). In terms of cultural sensitivity and complexity, Parker raised awareness of the fact that NGOs themselves are becoming more internally complex in cultural terms requiring more attention to be paid to the management of diversity, which was referred by the author as an increasing feature of new management thinking within the private sector (1998).

In the *The PraxisNote N°1 – How Can Knowledge Transferability Be Managed Across Cultures?* (Jackson and Sorgenfrei, 2003) it was argued that cross-cultural management theory and approaches are central to NGO management and capacity building: "the way knowledge, technology and 'best practice' is transferred from one country to another may be problematic without considering the cross-cultural implications." Furthermore, cross-cultural may have consequences for the way NGOs import foreign management principles as well as the way organisational and project impact are assessed as concepts (including human values, exclusion, gender, and power) differ widely across cultures (Jackson and Sorgenfrei, 2003, p. 4).

The Guide to the PMD Pro developed by the PM4NGOs, goes further and highlights the importance of working with the existent cultural references:

> project managers should also possess the competency to work effectively within the culture of their own organisation. Can the project manager navigate his/her specific organisation's framework, organisational culture, business processes/systems and human resources networks? The organisation's culture defines its identify (brand) and distinguishes it from other organisations managing similar projects
>
> (PM4NGOs, 2013, p. 12).

Hailey proposes that the rigid approaches to participation in the work of NGOs could risk not only being culturally inappropriate but may be more threatening as part of the agenda of donor agencies (2001). This proposal was meant in a specific context of South Asia but it raises questions of the relevance of participative decision-making processes both in relation to the cultural context – what type of participation is culturally appropriate and why?

In this context, wider stakeholder involvement in decision-making processes is both more appropriate in the communalistic-oriented cultures and more effective in making suitable organisational decisions for sustainable development and capacity building. According to Jackson, embedding cultural references within a participatory leadership in NGOs is crucial as these references have implications (among other aspects) for management and staff motivation, an area neglected in the literature in views of cross-cultural (2003).

Community-level, nature-based and/or heritage tourism development invokes a need for inclusive participation (Cleaver, 1999; Scheyvens, 1999). However, the concept of participation as a grass-roots panacea to civic alienation and economic inequity has been critiqued for its overemphasis on technique, resulting in the prioritisation of efficiency over empowerment (Cleaver, 1999). A failure to address deeper social, political, and economic realities that differentially impact people's ability to participate in development initiatives has led to the neglect of power issues, as well as a lack of attention to the distribution of access and control of information and resources (Chabota and Duhaimea, 1998; Cleaver, 1999). To Jackson, participation could more usefully be seen as incorporating a range of stakeholders, including those within the community (2003).

In artistic projects aiming for social change, participation is a particularly dear tool to involve the audience in ways that make them/us aware of the power each citizen has in transforming society. What the short history of cross-cultural project management tells is that participation can be a key ingredient for success but a lot remains to be done to overcome the power structures that limit it.

Notes

1 This is reflected in the number of artists whose practice takes the form of using the body to communicate a message, as New York-based artist Yoko Ono, who invited the public to cut her clothes off (Cut Piece, 1964) claiming that "the artist's ego is in the artist's work. In other words, the artist must give the artist's ego to the audience" (Yoko Ono, 1964 – Yoko Ono Infinite at Universe Dawn. *Cut Piece, 1964*. Retrieved on 6 May, 2013, from http://onoverse.com/2013/02/cut-piece-1964/)
2 In September 2011, the exhibition Spectres of the Nineties at the Marres Centre for Contemporary Culture in Maastricht, curated by Lisette Smiths, in collaboration with Matthieu Laurette, proposed a reading of critical artistic practices of the 1990s, via a materialistic analysis (Larssen, 2012).
3 The Kunsthalle saw a change of context itself as it is a former butchers' market from the last century now converted into a gallery, a change that has become a common practice in the last decades as demonstrable in various art spaces as The Matadero, in Madrid and the Karriere, in Copenhagen, formerly a meat packing district (Kødbyen).
4 Beuys statement dated 1973, first published in English in Caroline Tisdall: *Art into Society, Society into Art* (ICA, London, 1974), p.48. Capitals in original.
5 A paraphrase of *Rachel Wetzler, ARTnews*, September 2015, p.20, under the title *Being a Good Critic in a Bad World.*
6 As the war-torn nations of Europe faced famine and economic crisis in the wake of World War II, the United States proposed to rebuild the continent in the interest of

political stability and a healthy world economy. On June 5, 1947, in a commence-ment address at Harvard University, Secretary of State George C. Marshall first called for American assistance in restoring the economic infrastructure of Europe. Western Europe responded favourably, and the Truman administration proposed legislation. The resulting Economic Cooperation Act of 1948 restored European agricultural and industrial productivity. Credited with preventing famine and political chaos, the plan later earned General Marshall a Nobel Peace Prize.

7 Although little distinction is clearly stated between multi-, inter-, and trans-dis-ciplinary inquiry many would argue that there is a significant difference: "Trans-disciplinary approaches involve multiple disciplines **and** the space between the disciplines **with** the possibility of new perspectives 'beyond' those disciplines. Where multidisciplinary or interdisciplinary inquiry may focus on the contribution of dis-ciplines to an inquiry transdisciplinary inquiry tends to focus on the inquiry or issue itself" (Nicolescu, 1998). A transdisciplinary team would sit together from the first step of the discussion of the issues under debate and come up, together, with a solution. A multidisciplinarity team would sit separately and, in different stages, join the efforts, visions, and knowledge of each discipline.

8 Articles in the 1983 *Journal of Communications* issue on Ferment in the Field (Vol. 33, No 3 [Summer 1983]) noted a bifurcation of the field between a culturalist approach and more empirical approaches in the study of mass-mediated commu-nications. Topics in this area included analysis of the political economy of the media, audience reception and study of media effects, media history, the interaction of media institutions with other domains of society, and the like. Kellner (1995) made analyses of how the Frankfurt school, British cultural studies, and French postmodern theory all overcome the bifurcation of the field of culture and com-munications into text- and humanities-based that might be seen as multidisciplinary approaches.

9 Luhmann considers the concept of the world as a concept paradox that always represents a combination of determination and indetermination, unit and difference. The world is then seen as a unit of the past and the future, observer and observed one, Ego and Alter Ego (Corsi, Sposito, and Baraldi, 1996).

2 Disciplines and their perspectives
Art, cultural studies, and project management on social change

Art meets cultural studies: art making as a human behaviour

In this research, the interest in the link between art and cultural studies was first due to the observation that many art projects for social change seem to overlook the existent cultural references of the communities subject to the projects and this might be one of the causes for failure. During the research path, some concepts indicated that there might be more similarities than expected between different disciplines – such as art, cultural studies, and project management – even if these concepts are understood from different perspectives. From this observation it became relevant to find out if there are historical links (and what these would be) between art and cultural studies.

According to Malchiodi, and as already mentioned, art making is considered to be a universal human behaviour, which has always been a part of our personal and interpersonal communication (2007). This implies that art and culture are linked since art's inception as art is considered one part of human communication (following ideas such as the previously observed Luhmannian concept of art as social system) and, therefore, art is related to the cultural context and meanings where it is made and communicated. This is not to say that communication needs art but that art implies human communication.

In the last decade, university degrees addressing both art and culture have been proliferating. In general terms, such programmes investigate the relationship between art, society, and various aspects of the media as well as the methods that shape both art and society within its economic and political meanings. The approaches of these programmes are usually announced as either transdisciplinary or multidisciplinary and it seems that the differences between the two concepts are not fully understood and applied. The concepts are mentioned as part of the programmes' approach but are not justified or explained further than combining disciplines. These programmes claim to be designed to attract students interested in examining the relations between society and various media in depth and detail, but they seem themselves to lack depth and detail in understanding the very basics of putting together different disciplinary discourses, knowledge, and interests as they do not partner with other universities with expertise in the areas they do not have (an Arts College partnering with an Economics School would be an example). The lack of such collaborations indicates that much remains to be explored' or 'known' in terms of fully understanding and integrating different discourses and their relationships.

Nevertheless, the creation of such university programmes shows a growing interest in the study of the relationships between different disciplinary discourses, such as culture and art. Cultural studies is seen in the light of these programmes as a tool to foster critical thinking about the social and political significance of cultural objects, forms, and processes and some of these objects or cultural artefacts are art and design objects. The main problem with these university programmes seems to be that they are mainly theoretical. It seems necessary and enriching to observe and learn what has been made, in theory, to be able to make something new. But is that enough? In many projects initiated by artists only or even by a multidisciplinary team, there seems to be a lack of understanding of the culture of the community and embedding the existing cultural references proved to be difficult through observation only, as will be further presented and analysed through the case studies in the following chapter. Therefore, even though these university courses might be good research tools to address questions and improve research, maybe they could evolve if there was a clear understanding of the flaws and gaps of implementing a multidisciplinary project, in practical terms.

Studies in linking art and cultural studies question dominant assumptions and engage with important cultural controversies, especially around questions of value and the distribution of power and authority, which relates to the importance of the culture of the community and embedding the existing cultural references. Here it is important to go back to the theoretical discourses of the disciplines of art, cultural studies, and project management, where the idea of empowerment arises.

There is a growing literature concerning empowerment, participation, and art projects, and some practical researches deal directly with art projects as anti-poverty initiatives. Arsenault (n/d) has examined relationships of young people's poverty, representation, and power, specifically exploring performing arts as a point of activation for self-expression, self-realization, agency, and activism. This relates both to art and cultural studies as it implies that when making an art project for social change, there is a need to consider cultural, political, and ethical considerations involved in helping relationships. The projects put the focus on integrating experience with theoretical understandings of power as it relates to race, class, gender, and other social categories.

Materialist and art theories provide important lenses for work in the field of cultural studies and focus critical questions on the production, consumption, and distribution of objects and their actual and perceived meanings. The study of cultural theory facilitates an understanding of the dynamics between art and culture, individual and society, and generates insight into how social differences such as race, ethnicity, class, and gender shape and unsettle cultural production and consumption as well as perception. The study of cultural theory also inevitably raises the question of social change and its meaning.

An early example of the relationship between culture (as culture of a society) and art is illustrated in the Manifesto for an Independent Revolutionary Art (Breton and Rivera, 1938). According to the Manifesto, art could only exist in the context of a free society that shows an activist response towards exploitation and domination and where individuals can freely associate themselves and determine themselves. Here, the relationship between art and politics as well as between art and the culture of a society shows itself strongly in a denouncement of fascism and Stalinism, two dictatorships suffocating artistic expression. The manifesto opposed the abstract idea that art could somehow be neutral in a class-based society.

Jumping five decades to the Luhmannian idea of art as a social system, art echoes and comments on society through its perceptions of reality. The change of perception (self-perception and also the perception of a grand narrative) through alternative narratives is a methodology dear to many contemporary artists. In *A Few Howls Again* (2010), by Silvia Kolbowski (b.1953, Argentina), the life of journalist Ulrike Meinhof (1934–1976) is retold. Meinhof was a founding member of the Red Army Faction (RAF; Rote Armee Fraktion), a German extreme left-wing group that used terrorism in the struggle against what it claimed to be the violence of a capitalist and fascist society. The story of this group as it stands immortalised in the Museum of German History in Berlin recounts that Meinhof was arrested, together with the other leaders of the group's first generation in 1972, and was found hanged in her cell in 1976. In *A Few Howls Again*, the story is different: Meinhof appears with a gash to her throat, suggesting that she was murdered instead of the suicide recounted in historical documents. In dialogues and silent confrontations, the past is brought into the present.

Ai Weiwei is an outstanding case of the powerful use of narratives as an artistic and activist tool. Ai Weiwei works in a broad spectrum of art forms, such as photography, sculpture, installation, and whatever fits best the translation of the contemporary world as he sees it. But more than anything, his way of perceiving and communicating the world conceives all these genres together in an overall practice, where the medium immediately encountered by the audience always turns out sharply to indicate, more than art forms, stories which are – in his works – embedded in the contemporary social realm. Rather than presenting us grand narratives of the world – particularly of China but also of other parts of the world, specifically Europe, as his recent body of work tells and on which this text will focus – Ai's works greet us with small stories and voices that are usually silenced. This is particularly visible in his body of work addressing migration and identity such as *Fairytale* (2007), his project for Documenta 12, in which he sent 1,001 Chinese citizens to Kassel, in Germany. Through this project, more than showing an image of identity processes through history, Ai mimicked a process that puts people going through the system, with its complexities. Each participant in *Fairytale* was asked to fill out a form with almost 100 questions and was filmed before, during the trip, and after returning to China by Ai Weiwei's professional documentary team. With this methodology, the 1,001 small stories of each person as single individuals, with their backgrounds, fantasies, and hopes are documented, rather than ideas of one mass or collective identity of a country.

These practices and uses of narrative contradict Georg Lukács' position. He argues that reality exists objectively and independently of consciousness, and, therefore, cognition would be a reflection of reality. In the same way, art would have to be a factual reflection of the totality of reality, providing an image of reality where the opposition between essence and appearance of reality is given in a natural unity. Each artwork would have to be a closed universe that advances a more complete and livelier reflection of reality than the recipients have, it would have to seize the shiftiness and inexhaustibility of reality. For doing so, the role of art would not be to portray individual persons and situations, but representative characters under archetypal social and cultural contexts. Art would have to communicate a vast expression of the experiences of life, and, in this process, it would require a propaganda character (Lukács, 1954, p. 277).

When looking at the idea of art as social practice, it is not so much about the perception that art gives about reality, society, and the world but more a matter of regarding art as something inherent to culture. Bourriaud considers his idea of relational aesthetics to be a means of locating contemporary practice within the culture at large (1998). Marcellini and Rana (2012) have acknowledged that social practice has also been positioned "in the areas of spatial practice, artistic research, experimental geography, performance art, dance, and theatre" (p. 286). They argue "despite widespread contention over its origins, there is a growing consensus that the artistic field of social practice is defined by a focus on working with human subjects" (p. 286). The common ground in the theoretical framework that shapes the term social practice across exhibitions, academic programmes, and research is the relationship between art and society, both at an individual and collective level.

Bourriaud is concerned with the role of art in society in terms of art history, and, despite showing an interesting perspective, it is rather closed to the art world and, paradoxically, seems to fall out of where it claims to be located: the social realm. Maria Lind, in her essay for the exhibition's catalogue of *Living as Form* (2011), goes further and shows a concern with the correlations between art, culture, and society – Lind argues that "artists have long desired that art enter life" (Lind, 2011) emphasising art's sustained interest in social, political, and cultural changes. In the context of Maria Lind's text and in this research, culture is seen as in the definition created by Kroeber and Kluckhohn based on the idea that behaviour is both acquired and transmitted by symbols, constituting the distinctive achievement of human groups, including their embodiment in artefacts. An essential core of culture consists of traditional values, culture is the mix between ideas, values, and behaviours (Kroeber and Kluckhohn, 1952).

Lind's view is of the artist as a citizen who can communicate a message and ask for participation but in some cases, go further and take real political action. This does not mean that all artists need or should take political action or have a role in the culture of a society, in terms of the ways it is made and perceived. In the same way not all citizens are activists, not all artists need, want, or have to be activists.

Both the history of art and the history of cultural studies put the emphasis on participation and on audience. Therefore, it is important to see how both Histories look at it. When looking at the history of cultural studies, with its postmodern turn, there is an increasing emphasis on the audience: how audiences produce meanings and how cultural texts produce both popular pleasures and forms of resistance (Fiske, 1989a, 1989b). In the history of art, in postmodern times, there was also a turn to the audience as pointed out by theoreticians such as Nicolas Bourriaud (1998) and artists such as Joseph Beuys, with his social sculpture.

In cultural studies, audiences are seen as producers of meanings, and cultural texts might produce both popular pleasures and forms of resistance. Participation is therefore seen as a catalyst for self-development involving connections with other people, organisations, and institutions, in particular those that involve shared power and decision-making. As such, the act of participation moves people from being passive objects to subjects active in the managing of development within their communities.

In art, participation is seen in a more radical way as it implies a full involvement and, to some extent, a utopian vision of creating a dynamic that would draw the attention of everybody and would make everybody participate, one way or another. The dominant narrative of the history of socially engaged, participatory art across the 20th century is one in which the activation of the audience is positioned against its mythic counterpart, passive spectatorial consumption. Participation thus forms part of a larger narrative that traverses modernity: "art must be directed against contemplation, against spectatorship, against the passivity of the masses paralysed by the spectacle of modern life" (Groys, 2009). This desire to activate the audience in participatory art is at the same time a drive to emancipate it from a state of alienation induced by the dominant ideological order – be this consumer capitalism, totalitarian socialism, or military dictatorship. Beginning with this premise, participatory art aims to restore and realise a communal, collective space of shared social engagement. But this is achieved in different ways: either through constructivist gestures of social impact, which refute the injustice of the world by proposing an alternative, or through a nihilist redoubling of alienation, which negates the world's injustice and illogicality on its own terms. In both instances, the work seeks to forge a collective, co-authoring, participatory social body, but one does this affirmatively (through utopian realisation), the other indirectly (through the negation of negation). From the perspective of social sculpture, everything should be approached creatively and this would only be possible when all humans would consider themselves as artists, as creative agents of society. Beuys's utopic mission is "to build a social organism as a work of art," and to transform art into the "only evolutionary revolutionary power" (as cited in Bishop, 2006, p. 125).

Art history shows a rather utopian and extreme vision of what participation means, putting all the attention in the creativity and assuming that everybody can and wants to be active in society. In cultural studies there is a hierarchy implicit to participation: someone identifies a problem within a community and gathers a team to solve it, with the participation of the community.

Both cultural studies and art have been criticised for being populist, which was, possibly, a result of their ways of understanding participation. Critics of the phase of cultural studies known as postmodern claim that the project of this discipline has been losing its critical edge, has fallen into a postmodern cultural populism (McGuigan, 1992), and has surrendered the political radicalism and critical thrust of the original project (Kellner, 1995). Defenders of the turn towards cultural populism argue that the original, more critical model tended to be overly elitist and excessively critical of popular pleasures, while neglecting the complex ways that cultural texts can be appropriated and used.

Critics of relational aesthetics and participatory art, speak about a moment when an important sector of artists renounce the aesthetic vocabularies of contemporary art, claiming to be engaged in more serious, worldly, and political issues. Such anti-aesthetic refusals are not new: just as it is possible to recognise the Dada cabaret, situationist détournement, or dematerialised conceptual and performance art as having their own aesthetics of production and circulation, so too do the often formless-looking photo-documents of participatory art have their own experiential regime. The history of participatory art allows an understanding of the tension between equality and quality, between participation and spectatorship, and between art and real life. These conflicts indicate that social and artistic judgments do not easily merge; indeed, they seem to demand different criteria. This impasse surfaces in every printed debate and panel discussion on participatory and socially engaged art. For one sector of artists, curators, and critics, a good project appeases a super-ego injunction to ameliorate society; if social agencies have failed, then art is obliged to step in. In this schema, judgments are based on humanist ethics, often inspired by Christianity. What counts is to offer ameliorative solutions, however short-term, rather than to expose contradictory social truths. For another sector of artists, curators, and critics, judgments are based on a sensible response to the artist's work, both in and beyond its original context. In this schema, ethics are nugatory, because art is understood continually to throw established systems of value into question, including morality; devising new languages with which to represent and question social contradiction is more important. The social discourse accuses the artistic discourse of amorality and inefficacy, because it is insufficient merely to reveal, reduplicate, or reflect upon the world; what matters is social change. The artistic discourse accuses the social discourse of remaining stubbornly attached to existing categories and focusing on micro-political gestures at the expense of sensuous immediacy (as a potential locus of disalienation). Either social conscience dominates, or the rights of the individual to question social conscience. The relationship of art to the social is either underpinned by morality or it is underpinned by freedom.[1]

Both critics of the phase of cultural studies known as postmodern and critics of the phase of art known as participatory or relational aesthetics (in the postmodern) claim that the project of the disciplines, with its focus on participation, has fallen into populism and is missing a critical approach. In cultural studies, the claim by the critics is that the discipline is losing its critical edge and, in art, that the discipline is losing its aesthetic concern in favour of the relationship with society.

Looking at the early history of cultural studies and a possible link with the history of art, the oppositional and emancipatory potential of avant-garde art movements was a primary emphasis of the Frankfurt School, especially Adorno and Walter Benjamin during the 1930s, but British and North American cultural studies have largely neglected engaging avant-garde art forms and movements (McGuigan, 1997). Many versions of cultural studies and the sociology of culture overlooked a possible development of philosophical perspectives on aesthetics as is found in the Frankfurt School. But the rejection of high culture, modernism, and aesthetics also points in British cultural studies to a failure to develop a radical cultural and media politics, such as is found in the works of Brecht and Benjamin, concerned with activist and participatory cultural politics and the development of alternative oppositional cultures (Brecht, 1930/1983). The ignoring of modernist and avant-garde art and intense focus on the popular was aided and abetted by the postmodern turn in cultural studies which disseminated key positions and strategies of British cultural studies throughout the world but also helped produce an important mutation in cultural studies (Kellner, 1998).

In the same way production, distribution, and consumption of culture were, in earlier models of cultural studies, contextualised to critically analyse cultural texts, the making of art and visual culture were contextualised and influenced by left-wing political values such as collectivism, equality, and the search for alternative economies to critically analyse social behaviour and, more loosely, society. The direct involvement of visual artists in politics and the social and ethical values of left-wing politics can be traced to the French Revolution, when artists such as Jacques-Louis David granted permission for their artwork to be reproduced to support the Republican cause. This involvement might be seen as a claim about the ability of art to deliver political and social change, or instead an observation on the effect political values have had on the processes, aesthetics, and display of artworks made in a social and political context (Manacorda, 2013).

If the attempt to trace a relationship between cultural studies and social theory as well as the relationship between cultural studies and art has shown anything, it is that this is a shifting, non-linear, and variable one.

Art meets project management: creativity, chaos, and complexity from two perspectives

In this research, the link between art and project management was the subject of study for two different reasons. First, the observation that many art projects for social change overlook practical, planning, and strategic aspects and the hypothesis is that this might be one of the causes for failure. Second, during the review of literature presented in the previous chapter, concepts such as empowerment and participation appeared both in art and project management. Other concepts that come across in both disciplinary discourses are creativity, chaos, and complexity. Nevertheless, the ways these concepts are translated differ from one discourse to the other.

Even though there is a growing interest in management as the proliferation of postgraduate degrees in the area of arts management and the spread of toolkits for art and culture show, there is a deficit of practical advice on the role of, and skills needed in order to undertake project management within the discipline of art. In the last two decades, there has been some study of the multidisciplinary in the realms of art and project management. Yet, the strategic relevance of multidisciplinarity in the context of projects for social change has seemingly not yet been applied methodologically (Hassard, 1993) and needs further study and research.

Despite the gaps and misunderstandings between art and project management, if there are concepts shared by both, it might be useful to look at the Histories of these disciplines to understand the origins of the grand narratives associated with both disciplinary discourses. Maybe both could benefit from a better understanding of each discipline's characteristics and potential combinations in projects.

At first sight, art and science look to be very separate disciplines as science is usually concerned with rationality and rigid methodology whereas art is usually related to subjectivity and chaos. It would then sound obvious that art and project management belong to separate worlds. Although, on closer inspection of the history of both disciplines, project management is often described as both a science and an art (Warburton and Kanabar, 2012) and, similarly, there has been a fascination of art towards science almost since its inception. This relationship between two apparently different worlds appears in the idea of social sculpture coined by Beuys in the 1970s: to Beuys, creativity was neither exclusive of artists, nor capital exclusive of corporations. To him, both were not only equally present but also available to all within their daily lives and practices.

Project management has shown interest in creativity, especially when it comes to complex projects and projects involving innovation or change. Traditionally, project management is bound to control, measurement, monitoring, and evaluation of the planning and execution of a project, its results, and the produced knowledge. In the context of innovative projects and projects for social change, the environment is often considered as unstable and dynamic;

processes of idea generation are complex and difficult to manage. Usually, the couple creativity and project management is considered a contradiction in itself (Gilson, Palmer, and Schneider, 2005). Creativity aims at improving efficiency in problem solving; creativity is considered as a pillar of organisational change and the foundation of innovation. Project management refers to the standardisation of procedures and working practices with the objective to optimise organisational, control, monitoring, and evaluation performances. Midler and Lenfle (2003) describe the evolution of project management and identify gaps in a conventional mode of rationalisation of breakthrough innovations. In their recent work, Cohendet and Simon (2007) developed the relationship between knowledge, creativity, innovation, and projects as social dynamics. In this way, they reconsider and redefine the creative process. Whereas creativity in the Arts is usually regarded as a driving force for change and perception, a possible definition of creativity, in the context of project management, could be problem solving and knowledge creation (Cohendet and Simon, 2007) in badly known, unpredictable, and unknown contexts. Creativity involves "break thinking" (Hatchuel, Masson, and Weil, 2011) compared to known, controlled, and manageable contexts. Until now, tools for increasing creativity have been proposed but a comprehensive approach is still lacking (Cullman, 2013). Industry, not just the creative industry, is looking for aid to the implementation and optimisation of creative teams. Non-creative industries especially require approaches for the lack or absence of idea generation, management of the unknown, and permanent change.

In the same way that, at first, the connection between project management and creativity might sound unusual, at first sight, the link between art and science is also not obvious. Although, in the 15th century, in Italy, Leonardo da Vinci (1452–1519) was making drawings of the human body where the scientific detail of the anatomic observation was as remarkable as the mastery of the drawing technique in creating the illusion of three dimensions. Circa 1490, Leonardo da Vinci managed to visually translate the methods of the work of Roman architect and engineer Vitruvius who had already tried to inscribe the proportions of the human body to a square and a circle but without success. With what would become known as the Vitruvian Man, Leonardo da Vinci methodically determined the perfect fit of the body in mathematical patterns in a drawing that turned out to be an icon for the basic symmetry of the human body and, as a consequence, of the universe.

It is also unavoidable to mention his plans, experiences, and methods for flying machines, with a detail and rigour that resemble more a representation of something existent than the fruit of an idea. These projects, in the 15th century considered as utopias, are today seen both as art, due to the perfection of the drawing, and experiences that are inspiring for scientific disciplines such as mechanical engineering.

Four centuries later, on the 20th February 1909, Filippo Marinetti would publish the Futurist Manifesto in ecstasy at the technical evolution.

We declare that the splendour of the world has been enriched by a new beauty: the beauty of speed. A racing automobile with its bonnet adorned with great tubes like serpents with explosive breath ... a roaring motor car which seems to run on machine-gun fire, is more beautiful than the Victory of Samothrace."

(Marinetti, 1909)

Naturally, Marinetti was not alone, and his example was followed by many other artists whose production manifested in a clear tendency to praise the speed of the future. More than the celerity of the world, what interested artists who succeeded Marinetti lay in the understanding of the past in order to gain a perspective on the future, in a critical analysis of the moment in which they were living.

In contemporary art, many examples unfold in this fascination for science. That is the case – to name one example – of Miguel Palma, whose constructions begin with experiences articulated skilfully between the worlds of art, the everyday, science, and engineering. In experiences resulting from observations of situations and objects, he alters it adding layers of meaning. What started as a shipping container (*Air Print*, 2012) became a mechanical lung which, miraculously, sucks the polluted air of a city, and what could stay as a vitrine (*Carbono 14*, 1998) was transformed in a capsule containing a subterranean city, visible by a geological cut showing cars, sewers, segments of roads, and even interiors of houses, all being cultivated by an agriculture machine. In *Catalytic Paintings* (2007) the relationship between art and science is also evident in a mechanical process created to represent a landscape, a recurrent theme in the history of art, here revealed by a device. In 1993, Miguel Palma worked with a team of engineers to build a car (*Device*, 1993). Even written it sounds impossible. When we think of cars, we think of complex machines. We know how to use them but we do not know all of their components and how these are articulated and we certainly know that these machines are not handmade one by one. Miguel Palma challenges these preconceived notions of what is and what is not possible and deconstructs, in an interrogative look, the complexity of machines in an approximation to the human.

In the same way that putting art and science in the same phrase is not easy, thinking simultaneously in art and project management might appear as a contradiction per se. Nevertheless, if we look at art projects for social change, which might start with utopian ideas, we understand that scientists are authors of many actions that without deep observation, study, experiences, technical work, management, planning, and strategy, would not be more than ideas and would be far off becoming a project. This is what happens with a lot of contemporary art projects for social change: they seem to lack time and financial resources dedicated to deep observation, study, experiences, technical work, management, planning, and strategy. In short, they lack project management in their development and implementation.

Seeing these similarities contradicting grand narratives, it seems necessary to first explore the links between the Histories of the disciplines. Looking, for example, at the history of project management and art history with social issues, it is possible to understand the extent of participation and collaboration changing in the history of the discipline.

Participation, in the Arts, has been reimagined at each historical moment as portrayed in Figure 2.1: from a crowd (1910s), to the masses/Dada movement (1920s), to the people/social sculpture (late 1960s/1970s), to the excluded (1980s), to community/relational aesthetics (1990s), to today's volunteers whose participation is continuous with a culture of reality television and social networking. From the audience's perspective, it is possible to chart this as a shift from an audience that demands a role (expressed as hostility towards avant-garde artists who keep control of the proscenium), to an audience that enjoys its subordination to experiences devised for them by an artist, to an audience that is encouraged to be a co-producer/co-creator/co-author of the work (and who, occasionally, can even get paid for this involvement). This could be seen as a heroic narrative of the increased activation and agency of the audience, but it might also be seen as a story of their ever-increasing voluntary subordination to the artist's will, and of the commodification of human bodies in a service economy (since voluntary participation is also unpaid labour). Co-creation has been a major issue in Europe. Creative Europe, "the European Commission's framework programme for support to the culture and audiovisual sectors"[2] encourages co-creation as a means of audience development, one of the main criteria for funding artistic and cultural projects. This seems to be a growing tendency with the emerging conflicts in Europe, which have brought up issues of multiculturalism and conviviality:[3]

> To contribute to audience development by helping European artists/cultural professionals and their works reach new and enlarged audiences and improve access to cultural and creative works in the European Union (hereafter 'the EU') and beyond with a particular focus on children, young people, people with disabilities and underrepresented groups, by engaging in new and innovative ways with audiences both to retain and

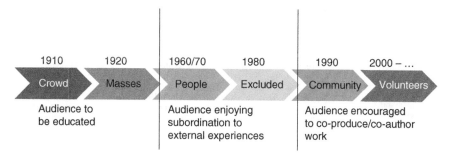

Figure 2.1 A history of participation in art

enlarge them, and to improve the experience and deepen the relationship with current and future audiences.[4]

(Creative Europe, 2015)

Moving on to the history of project management and its relationship with participation, it is important to note that this is a rather recent discipline. The appointment of people as project managers as a profession only started to emerge in the 20th century. In earlier times, the leadership of the project endeavour moved from a generalist role (17th century) held by the coordinating architects who were in charge of all aspects of design and delivery including cost control and time management; to more specialist roles and responsibilities assigned by contract in the 18th and 19th centuries to programme, and then project management in the 20th century. The 21st century is testimony to a series of new attempts of responses and meaningful ways on how to deal with complexity and cultural differences as cross-cultural complex project management. Figure 2.2 shows this evolution.

By the 18th century, the professions of (design) engineer and architect had evolved into professional organisations and those who built the projects were contractually and organisationally separate from the designers showing hierarchy and a low level of collaboration and participation between and from different disciplines.

The scientific knowledge of management progressed through the 19th and 20th centuries in response to forms of innovation in business and society. Modern project management uses many of the ideas and techniques developed from these growing, broad management concepts and experiences. The Industrial Revolution brought about the emergence of large-scale businesses with an intrinsic need for professional managers with specific knowledge in opposition to the use of generic and broad concepts.

In Raymond E. Miles' book *Theories of Management: Implications for Organisational Behaviour* (1975), a model of the evolution of management theory in the United States was interpreted. His model includes three management phases: classical; human relations; and human resources management. The origin of the ideas that guided the development of modern project management can possibly be traced back to the protestant reformation of the 15th century.[5] The Protestants and later the Puritans introduced a number of ideas including reductionism,[6] individualism,[7] and the protestant work ethic

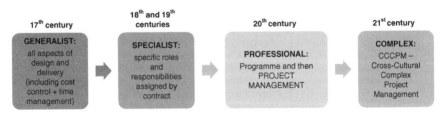

17th century	18th and 19th centuries	20th century	21st century
GENERALIST: all aspects of design and delivery (including cost control + time management)	**SPECIALIST:** specific roles and responsibilities assigned by contract	**PROFESSIONAL:** Programme and then PROJECT MANAGEMENT	**COMPLEX:** CCCPM – Cross-Cultural Complex Project Management

Figure 2.2 From generalist PM to CCCPM

(PWE)[8] that reverberate powerfully in the essence of modern project management. From the perspective of the evolution of modern project management, these ideas were assimilated into two main philosophies: Liberalism and Newtonianism (see Figure 2.3), which show different points of view towards participation and collaboration as well as towards society.

Whereas Liberalism, which goes back to the 18th century, included the ideas of capitalism (Adam Smith), the division of labour, and that an industrious lifestyle would lead to wealthy societies, Newtonianism marked the era of scientific enquiry. Liberalism advocated breaking the production of goods into tiny tasks that can be undertaken by people following simple instructions, without a specific or professional knowledge. An overall benefit for all was assumed, based on the concept that doing good and sympathy for others created happiness whilst rejecting them created misery. Therefore, the self-interest of the factory owner was synonymous with benevolence, and, as a consequence, directed his selfish interest to the benefit of society as a whole. Here it is possible to establish a comparison to the moments in art when artists ask people for participation in building a social organism for a better society (social sculpture advocated by Beuys) but the difference lies in giving tasks versus asking for participation in whatever task one person wants to do. Here, again, it is possible to see the planning and control of project management versus the seeming disorder of art. Maybe none is completely right as history shows many projects failing in both areas and maybe a possible solution would be the understanding and combination of both approaches.

Going back to Newtonianism, Newton had a view of the world as a sort of agreeable mechanism that was then controlled by a universal law. If one would apply scientific observations to parts of the whole, one would understand and insights would occur in what would eventually become a complete understanding of the Universe as a whole.

Robert Owen (1771–1858) and Charles Babbage (1792–1871) were two of the early management thinkers. Owen understood people should not be

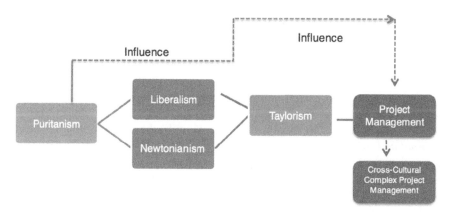

Figure 2.3 Evolution of modern project management (adapted from Wæver, 2007)

considered as simple machinery but people with desires and abilities and announced improved working conditions at his Scottish cotton mill. Similarly, Babbage was interested in work specialisation and motivation of individuals. This might have been the first step in the understanding of teamwork, collaboration, and participation in organisations, and, therefore, the importance of behavioural or human relations. To a larger extent, this has an impact both in the organisations and in the societies in which they act.

Behavioural or human relations management emerged in the 1920s, after World War I and dealt with the human aspects of organisations. It has been referred to as the neoclassical school because it began with a reaction to the weaknesses of the classical approaches to management. As in the discipline of art, the clash between artistic and social critiques recurs most visibly at certain historical moments, and the reappearance of participatory art is symptomatic of this clash; it seems that in project management the appearance of interest in human relations management tends to occur at moments of political transition and upheaval: in the aftermath of World War I and in the outcome of World War II. It might be interesting to look into the links between political transitions and their upheaval and how this is translated in and via different disciplines in social terms.

Beginning in the early 1950s, after World War II, the human resources school represented a substantial progression from human relations. The behavioural approach did not always increase productivity. Thus, motivation and leadership techniques became a topic of great interest. The human resources school understands that employees are very creative and competent, and that much of their talent is largely untapped by their employers. Employees want meaningful work; they want to contribute; they want to participate in decision-making and leadership functions.[9] Participation, as discussed before, is a cherished theme in the contemporary arts both in terms of relational aesthetics, initiated by the art world itself, and in a more spontaneous way, as an exploration of arts as a point of activation for self-expression, self-realisation, agency, and activism. Thus, even if at an unconscious and empirical level, motivation and leadership techniques became an issue in the Arts as they did in project management.

The evolution of project management seems to have mirrored the evolution in general management; starting with a focus on scientific processes in the early years, moving to a softer skills focus and a more holistic perception of a project in its specific social, cultural, and economic context, as the possible varied interests of project stakeholders in the 21st century. This trend is clearly demonstrated by analysis of papers published in the *International Journal of Project Management* which shows a drop from 49 to 12% for task-focused papers (scheduling, etc.), offset by increases in papers on subjects such as leadership, stakeholder, systemic, and complex cross-cultural management. Here it is possible to make a parallel with art as it has also been evolving from passive to active with art projects that touch and attempt to contribute to the complex issues raised in different social and cultural contexts. When creating such projects, artists need to look for stakeholders and it seems that there is an increasing interest in finding a compromise for what is best for the stakeholders, the artists, and those who are the subjects of the project.

In the relationship between art and project management, Thamhain (2002) compares project managers to a social architect whose major concern should be to understand and possibly change human behaviours through carefully designed projects that seek to involve through participation the members of a population to improve their own communities. The concept of social architect is not too distant from the idea of social sculptor advocated by art in its relationship with social change as both imply active community participation. The difference resides in the type of participation even though both advocate its importance (Figure 2.4): whereas a project manager as a social architect has a more influential role in the community as he is the one initiating and designing a project, under the concept of social sculpture, participation is a trope for social change within any community but any community member is seen equally as an artist and an active member with the same role in the community.

In recent history, project management evolved and became an autonomous discipline and profession: "Project management has been practiced for thousands of years since the Egyptian era, however, it has been about half a century ago that organisations start applying systematic project management tools and techniques to complex projects" (Carayannis, Kwak, and Anbari, 2005, p. 18). Snyder and Kline (1987) argue that modern project management began in 1958 with the development of CPM/PERT[10]. As for the origin of project management, Morris and Hough (1987) argues that its appearance goes back to the chemical industry just before World War II. Morris (1987) interestingly refers to project management as a clearly defined and separate discipline in the Atlas missile programme, especially in the Polaris project. Some literature pointed the origin of project management to Henri Fayol's (1916/1949) five functions of a manager: (1) to plan, (2) to organise, (3) to

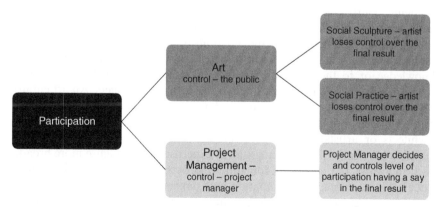

Figure 2.4 Participation/control in projects within art and project management

coordinate, (4) to control, and (5) to direct or command. Kerzner (1998) observes that project management is an "outgrowth of systems management." Looking at the history of contemporary art, which is not chronologically far from the history of modern project management, it is possible to observe that art has shown a renewed interest in scientific disciplines, ranging from engineering (in artists such as Miguel Palma, Simon Starling, and Gabriel Orzoco who work frequently together with engineers to produce their art projects) to social sciences such as in the 1970s concept of social sculpture and the 1990s idea of social practice, which is still a trend 20 years later as seen in the multiplicity of art projects for social change. Even though there is an interest expressed by art in scientific disciplines and methods including project management, it also dismisses an understanding of the evolution in the discipline of project management. Art projects for social change as well as other projects in the art domain claim to apply the knowledge of project management. The problem seems to be that there is not a full understanding of what project management might mean and imply and it is more seen and applied in art at a superficial level dismissing its evolution from an empirical application to a scientific discipline and profession. Another problem seems to be that art is reluctant to work within the world of profit[11] and, therefore, has a problem with being related to money. This is very problematic when making a project for social change as even when the projects do not require money, in most cases, they should be sustainable and when looking at social issues, it is difficult to avoid its relationship with economics and politics. Also, it is almost unavoidable to dismiss the financial part of a project whatever the goals and formats, as will be discussed further in the description of *Morrinho, Project Row Houses* and *Intervene: Heroes and Villains.*

In the recent history of art, there is a concern and interest in embedding the characteristics and methods of scientific disciplines, with a strong focus on project management. This is seen in various ways: from public art projects and museums hiring art project managers, to art projects for social change claiming to use project management in their methods, and in the creation of academic courses relating art and project management. Although, the interest and concern does not always show practical results and might be comparable to the situation observed in the relationship between NGOs and project management: art, as NGOs, seems to be, in many cases, fixed to the empirical knowledge or to the historical origins and applications of project management. In some cases, art curators are seen as project managers. An art curator can play the role of a project manager but if that is the case, there are methodologies that should be observed and analysed and not all art curators (or architects or artists) can be good project managers in art projects. Some curators have some project management expertise and can liaise more broadly with the artist and client, coordinating and managing the public art project, undertaking community consultation and stakeholder management, conducting risk assessment, and managing the artwork commissioning, timeframe, and budget. In theory, this might sound enough but when asking curators the meaning and methodologies of project management in their projects, it is very rare to find specific and detailed answers and there is a profound lack of professional knowledge of the methodologies of project management.

On a more positive note, there are many toolkits, especially in the UK and Canada, explaining the importance of project management in the Arts. Even though there is, in most cases, dismissal of the state of the art of project management as a discipline (most of these toolkits do not refer to PMI, for example), these toolkits are important for the improvement and development of art projects and they show the pillars of project management in a comprehensive way. The problem with most of these toolkits is that in trying to be comprehensive, they become rather simplistic and lack further explanations on the benefits of applying the methods presented.

Public Art Aberdeen[12] developed a toolkit

> to develop a systematic and considered approach to developing and funding public art projects within Aberdeen. The plan will offer a range of people access to guidelines that will encourage a process of "self developed" individual projects using good practice principles
> (Public Art Aberdeen, 2011, section Public Art Toolkit, paragraph 1)

This is one of the examples that show art acknowledging the importance of project management. Public Art Aberdeen mentions four stages (Developing the Project; Activating the Project; Creating the Project; After the Project), which is the equivalent to the Project life cycle. The problem with these stages is that they are presented at a rather superficial level and do not show practical methods in a detailed way, which could have been beneficial for a better understanding. It also lacks the acknowledgement of project management as a discipline and this makes a huge difference to someone reading the document as if there were references to literature and practical examples, the opportunity to learn more and apply knowledge in practical terms could increase. There is also an absence of reasoning for using these phases and this could be considered additional as it is not a toolkit made for people familiar with the methods and benefits of project management. The thorough understanding of a project life cycle is important because it demonstrates the logic that governs a project. It also helps in developing plans for carrying out the project. Pinto (2007) identified four distinct project life cycle phases: Conceptualisation, Planning, Execution, and Termination. Conceptualisation, to Pinto (2007) suggests the development of the initial aim and technical description of a project. In this phase, the extent of work is drawn, necessary resources as people, capital, and material are listed, and important organisational contributions or stakeholders identified. A study of feasibility is conducted at this stage to investigate whether the project can be continued or should be dismissed or changed. Planning is, therefore, according to Pinto (2007), the stage in which thorough specifications, schematic, schedules, and other plans are established. The project's resolution is further developed in a detailed way drawing the steps necessary to meet the project's objectives in this phase. At this stage, the individual pieces of the project, called work packages, are broken down, individual assignments made, and the process for completion clearly delineated. Project schedule, the practical work, and the estimated cost of completion are also planned. At this stage, all envisioned threats to the successful completion of the project should be identified. According to Patel, the project stakeholders for the project must be identified at this stage in order to establish a communication plan, describing information needed and the delivery method to keep stakeholders informed of the project's progress and achievements (2008).

To Pinto, the execution phase deals with tangible performance of the work of the project. Progress is monitored and evaluated in a continuous way and appropriate adjustments are made, if needed, and variances are recorded in order to maintain the original project plan. During project execution, project tasks are carried out and progress information is being reported through regular team meetings (2007). This information is used to maintain control over the direction of the project by quantifying the performance of the project activities comparing the results with the project plan and corrective actions might be taken if necessary (Westland, 2003). The termination phase takes place when the finished project is transmitted to the customer, the project documentation is given to the business, the suppliers' contracts are terminated, the project resources are freed, and the project closure is communicated to all stakeholders. The final step is to conduct lesson learned studies, which can be described as an examination of what went well and what did not, in order to apply that knowledge in a future project. With this kind of analysis, the wisdom of experience is transferred back to the project organisation, which will help future management teams.

In art, despite some scarce good examples, the implementation of modern project management tools, methods, and techniques is still not well-established in projects, including projects for social change (mainly made in the frame and context of NGOs), which show a high degree of complexity. This results in failure of project initiators (be it NGOs, artists, museums, or public institutions) and their contractors in performing their duties concerning the budget, specifications, and deadlines of the projects awarded.

Even though it is clear that there is great effort in embedding knowledge of project management in art projects, there is also much work to be done and these projects could benefit tremendously from the application of professional modern project management methods and techniques. Studies have confirmed that application of professional modern project management methods and techniques applied thoroughly and rigorously have a great effect on public institutions (which is the case of *Intervene: Heroes and Villains)* and NGOs (as is the case of *Morrinho*). Arnaboldi, Azzone, and Savoldelli (2004) observed that application of project management strategy in the public sector was as a result of pressure on governments to abandon bureaucratic organisation in favour of leaner structures. The authors studied the projects carried out at the Italian Treasury Ministry using project management methodology and discovered that proper implementation of project management concepts and methods will help in avoiding project failure, continuous communication, and the definition of project control system. They, however, stated that, project management methods needed to be modified and specifically tailored towards the needs of public institutions. In a study carried out by White and Fortune, in 2002, current project management practice in the public sector in the UK was examined by collecting data from 236 project managers in some public institutions. The study asked the respondents to judge the effectiveness of the project management methods, tools, and techniques they had used on successful projects. The result of the study revealed that 41% of the reported projects were judged to be completely successful (using time, budget, and specification), though some drawbacks were reported. Similarly, Abbasi and Al-Mharmah (2000) explored the project management tools and techniques used by the public sector in Jordan by surveying 50 industrial public firms. The study found that the use of project management tools and techniques among the public sector companies was considerably low, but when practiced efficiently would result in tangible benefit in all aspects of planning, scheduling, and monitoring of time, cost, and specifications of projects.

Most activities in arts and culture happen in the framework of project management. In a simplified summary, exhibitions, activities, events, happenings, social practice, and projects for social change are all events that need to be thoroughly planned within a budget and a timeframe. Project management should therefore be considered as one of the fundamentals of the successful management of the creative sector; crucial to the long-term sustainability of arts and culture and ensuring a sound and stable environment in which artists can be creative.

In a reciprocal relationship, businesses, policy makers, and academics have consistently made the case for the importance of creative disciplines as art and design as tools for innovation, productivity, and economic growth and, therefore, social change or improvement. Many have argued that art is a link between creativity and innovation: Sir George Cox in his "Review of Creativity in Business," the European Commission, Professor Swann in his paper for BIS and Sir James Dyson in his report for the Conservative Party. This research found that the use of art and design is linked to improved business performance in a number of ways including turnover, profit, and market share. Previous research has shown this: between 1995 and 2004, the share prices of design-conscious companies outperformed other firms by 200% (British Design Council, 2010). For every £100 a design-alert business spends on design, turnover increases by £225 (British Design Council, 2010). The performing and visual arts, broadcasting, film-making, writing, and design, for example, encompass a range of activities which are economic and need to be managed well to realise effective results and, this being so, knowledge of project management is needed to implement art projects. The same applies for art projects for social change as these involve activities that, even if not for profit, need to be managed well to be sustainable.

Chaos and complexity under the lenses of art and project management

Besides these historical links in participation and creativity, two concepts that come across in the discourses of both art and project management are chaos and complexity. But what is meant by these concepts? Deleuze and Guattari's idea of chaos might throw some light on this question. According to them, scientific disciplines primarily develop functions ("functives," formulae, algorithms) to address and exchange with chaos and the discipline of art elaborates, produces, and intensifies effects and perceptions as its mode of response to and contamination by chaos[13].

In 1916, one year after Einstein published his theory of relativity, the first Dada performance took place in Zurich. The Swiss bourgeoisie was treated to total chaos with a merry senselessness. While science created order in the surrounding universe, it was the task of the arts to bring chaos into the order, according to the philosopher Theodor Adorno in 1958.

Whereas in art, chaos is seen as a way to achieve order, in project management as in other scientific disciplines, chaos is seen in relation to complexity and the goal is to manage chaos. The literature review in the previous chapter tells that chaos theory (also known as complexity theory) was originally developed in the context of physical and biological sciences; Butler, in 1990, Merry, in 1995, and Radzicki, in 1998, among others, have noted that social, ecological, and economic systems also tend to be characterised by nonlinear relationships and complex interactions that evolve dynamically over time. This recognition has led to a surge of interest in applying complexity theory to a number of fields, including medicine (Goldberger et al., 1990), international relations (Mayer-Kress and Grossman, 1989), and economics (Kelsey, 1988).

In a way, both art and scientific disciplines are looking to find order through chaos. Chaos in a dynamic project management system can be defined as: an unpredictable or disorderly event; an event that renews and revitalises the process; small changes in initial conditions leading to enormous consequences; similar patterns that take place across layers (fractal geometry); decisions need to be made even in the absence of all intended information. Controlling chaos by "shoehorning" it into a specific structure might not yield the desired results for an organisation (Wheatley, 1999). The first line of defence in order to manage chaos is a good management team and an even better project manager. An organisation can manage its chaos by seeking out the factors that are easiest to change (Bertelsen and Koskela, 2003). An organisation should then handle project dynamics and stress in the face of uncertainties. Finally, a manager should both always have a contingency plan and be able to keep track of critical factors and issue warnings. A learning ambience in the organisation or team helps in successful management of chaos (Bertelsen and Koskela, 2003).

In contemporary art, there are various artists developing work based on chaos theory. One example comes from Electronic Shadow (an artist duo composed of architect Naziha Mestaoui and multimedia director Yacine Aït Kaci) who connects sciences, art, and philosophy, conceiving a personal and subjective language, using technologies to design emotions and experiences for the audience. *Chaos Theory* is one of their last participatory pieces slightly inspired by a moment of their show *Double Vision* created with Carolyn Carlson in 2006. In accordance with their idea of chaos theory, the installation evolves from one exhibition to another and it is a completely renewed version in each place. Inspired by the scientific universe, as many of their previous installations (such as *Superfluidity*, 2009), their *Chaos Theory* explores the impossibility of predicting what comes next and the exponential amplification of errors or lapses of memory.

The inspiration from the scientific domain is clear but it is an interpretation revealing of the attempts at integration of scientific theories in art. Although, it is also important to acknowledge that there are many differences in meanings and perceptions when referring to the same concepts under different contexts and disciplines.

Philosophy invents concepts to create consistency from chaos, science functions to slow down chaos in order to extract from it limits, constants, measurements – variables it can use to generate predictabilities,[14] and the art's frame or compose chaos so that sensation can be created and proliferate. Each has its own engagements and struggles with chaos, each takes with it little shards of chaos through which it wrenches a consistency, an intensity, or a predictability in order to set itself on the other side of chaos, in order to compose, calculate, or conceptualise, but all have approaches in relation to chaos which can be complementary as all are looking for ways to achieve or interpret order.

The idea that science is an objective discipline that must isolate itself from social concepts like constructivism and relativism in order to function is dismissed by Porush, who notes that those who maintain the "canons of objectivity and impersonality are still hostile" to alternative approaches to the practice of science. He asserts that personal and political reasons, rather than academic reasons, explain why Prigogine has been positioned on the periphery of chaos theory by some of his colleagues (1993). With reference to Gaston Bachelard's perception of scientific discourse, Andrew Gibson argues in his book *Towards a Postmodern Theory of Narrative*, "Science constantly resorts to the imagination and traffics in the world of images, in a discourse that is radically other to the discourse that it tells us is its own" (Gibson, 1996, p. 120). A literary interpretation of the discourse of chaos theory indicates that it does not differ substantially from the subjective standards and modes of discourses of social sciences such as cultural studies and art. Even though the way the same concepts are seen under each discipline shows various differences, it also indicates points in common that can easily be dismissed in a first reading.

Despite the distinctive ways of looking at the same concepts, the understanding and integration of both can add value as each one allows for a different and new perspective. It is also interesting to note that the common assumptions that art is not able to operate within order and that project management kills the magic of creativity, or is not interested in it, are wrong assumptions.

Cultural studies meets project management: common characteristics to the contemporary society

Anbari et al. draw attention to the fact that project managers in the contemporary, multicultural, global business community are often faced with cultural differences (2004). These differences can boost but also inhibit the success and even the completion of the projects. The foundation of cross-cultural project management as a field of research (being in itself a PhD programme) that brings together young scholars from different academic and professional backgrounds ranging from arts, history, design, and project management translates how cultural differences are central to projects. Initiated in 2009 by the Berlin-based, consulting think-tank SE Group with the support of the European University of Viadrina (Frankfurt-Oder, Germany), CCCPM is a thought-provoking attempt to explore unconventional perspectives on the narratives of project management regarding social complexity in terms of culture and politics.

While there have been many studies that address the importance and role of culture in project management, there is very little literature addressing the role of culture in the project management processes and methodologies across different cultures. Thamhain compares project managers to social architects whose major concern is to understand and to change human behaviours through carefully designed projects that seek to involve the members of a population to improve their own communities (2002). Even though the role of culture is mentioned in the project management literature, it is not explored in depth and there is a lack of understanding of what the disciplines of cultural studies and project management could learn from each other.

The literature contains considerable empirical research on the management–culture relationship. Hofstede proposed that each culture has a favourite coordination mechanism, suggesting that people from each nation are able to perform more efficiently when using their own favourite management practices or, in other words, their own management and cultural references (Hofstede, 1991). In a similar study from 1996, Newman and Nollen made an empirical investigation, based on data from 176 work units in one large, American-based corporation with units located in 18 European and Asian countries. This study investigated the result of Hofstede's (1991) five national culture dimensions and their corresponding management practices.

Many project managers engaged in international and multidisciplinary projects would agree that project management is influenced by culture. Exactly how culture affects management, however, is a question that most would find difficult to answer. In collaborative, international, multidisciplinary teams there are several national cultures inherent to the professional, social, and economic backgrounds present which results in heterogeneous teams rather than homogenous groups. In previous analysis, culture gaps have been identified as a potential reason for project failure. This is especially evident for project management practices developed in Western cultures applied to projects in developing countries in different cultural contexts (Muriithi and Crawford, 2003). In their culture-related literature review, pointing out the relevance of culture when implementing a project, Henrie and Sousa-Poza analyse leading peer-reviewed project management journals and recently published project management books with a focus on culture within the project management discipline. In their analyses, they conclude that cultural knowledge and awareness is significant for project management professionals but also that empirical research on culture and project management continues to be limited (Henrie and Sousa-Poza, 2005).

Culture and the management of cultural differences are recognised as key influencing factors for virtual project teams. Crossing national boundaries entails the need to go beyond both tangible and intangible difficulties where one of the implicit obstacles is culture (Kliem, 2004). This is an idea that might be applied to the realm of disciplines as each disciplinary discourse holds a specific culture. Therefore, cultural knowledge and awareness of the existent cultural references have a significant role for project management professionals (Henrie and Sousa-Poza, 2005). The current state of research regarding project management in general and especially international project management shows that there currently is little knowledge in terms of its relationship with culture and cultural studies as a discipline. However, it seems that negative or positive impact of projects is highly dependent on the understanding of the multiple cultural references implied in each project (Henrie and Sousa-Poza 2005).

In project management, an effective communications plan and a common understanding of project objectives are critical issues and, at the same time, difficult challenges. All these issues are related to a sound project management methodology and the organisational environment of a project. While these aspects are still important in the context of multidisciplinary projects, the analysis of projects such as *Morrinho, Project Row Houses* and *Intervene: Heroes and Villains* indicate that there are even more important issues that refer to more intangible features of communication rooted in cultural differences. The differences in behaviours and attitudes, mentalities, and personalities as well as different interpretations of apparently simple questions such as what change is in fact required, need to be managed appropriately for project success.

The basis for effective cultural management seems then to be the ability to be aware of cultural differences and their relevance for managing people and project teams. Furthermore, experience with different people and cultures appears to be critical to obtain cultural fluency in the long run, which points to the need for mediation. This mediator role should be based on sound cultural fluency within the cultures involved. The number of cultures involved is not necessarily high, except for international projects. Domestic or community-based projects such as *Morrinho* show different cultures not only due to the various disciplines involved at a later stage of the Project but also because the team is composed of a large group of people with diverse backgrounds. Furthermore, the team is always in contact with international stakeholders and the project holds an international scope. The analysis of the three projects in the following chapter show that part of their success is due to the embedding and integration of existent cultural references. Many projects seem to fail because they overlook existent cultural references and the actual needs of the community, as seen in the difficulties faced by *Intervene: Heroes and Villains* and *Project Row Houses*, further analysed in Chapter 3.

The experts seem to agree that cultural awareness is mandatory, if not critical, in multidisciplinary project management (Houghton et al., 2013) and many agree that international projects bear additional risks compared to domestic and community-based ones (Baum, 1997). This poses distinct leadership challenges for project managers. Additional challenges for project managers result from integrating different communication patterns, behaviours, and attitudes into one functioning project team. The analysis of *Morrinho* presented in Chapter 3 shows that this integration is also needed in domestic or community-based projects.

Therefore, a project manager should be aware of existent (multiple) cultural references, both in international and domestic or community-based projects, including those for social change. This requires high levels of emotional intelligence including sensitivity to upcoming tensions or misunderstandings, respect for different approaches and narratives, and flexible adaptation to changing environments. In other words, the project manager should (also) be a mediator. But is it possible to fully understand cultural references that are not those of the mediator–project manager? How is a mediator–project manager regarded in a community being subjected to a project for social change? These questions might be better answered through projects and their narratives, such as the ones in the following chapter, rather than through theory.

Notes

1 Tony Bennett phrases the same problem differently: art history as a bourgeois, idealist discipline is in permanent conflict with Marxism as an anti-bourgeois, materialist revolution in existing disciplines. There is no possibility of reconciling the two. See Tony Bennett, *Formalism and Marxism* (London: Methuen, 1979), 80–85.
2 "Welcome to Creative Europe." Creative Europe. https://ec.europa.eu/programmes/creative-europe/ (accessed August 25th 2017).
3 In a recent amendment to the *Work Plan for Culture* (2015–2018) as regards the priority on intercultural dialogue, the European Commission has acknowledged that tackling the migration and refugee crisis is a common obligation which requires a comprehensive strategy and a determined effort over time in a spirit of solidarity and responsibility. Moreover, the amendment emphasises that "culture and the arts have their role to play in the process of integrating refugees who will be granted asylum status as they can help them to better understand their new

environment and its interaction with their own socio-cultural background, thus contributing to building a more cohesive and open society" (see http://data.con silium.europa.eu/doc/document/ST-14444-2015-INIT/en/pdf).

4 Creative Europe Culture Sub-programme: Support for European Cooperation Projects Guidelines 2015. Creative Europe. http://eacea.ec.europa.eu/sites/eacea -site/files/documents/guidelines-call-for-proposals-cooperation-projects-2015_en.pdf (accessed August 25th 2017).

5 Financial management is a key element of management control. Fra Luca Barto-lomeo de Pacioli published his treatise on double entry accounting in 1494, in Venice, which is the same bookkeeping system we use in the contemporary era. The ability to account effectively underpinned the success of Venice as a powerful trading state through the Renaissance and its spread certainly assisted in the development of companies during the Industrial Revolution.

6 Reductionism: removing unnecessary elements of a process or "ceremony" and then breaking the process down into its smallest task or unit to "understand" how it works.

7 Individualism: we are active, independent agents who can manage risks. These ideas are made into "real things" by social actions contingent upon the availability of a language to describe them.

8 PWE: prior to the protestant reformation most people saw work as a necessary evil (or at least as only a means to an end). For Protestants, serving God included participating in, and working hard at, worldly activities as this was part of God's design and purpose for each individual.

9 Some of the theories include: McGregor's theory "X" and theory "Y," theory "Z" (Ouchi), contingency theory (Morse and Lorsch), goal-setting theory (Latham and Locke) and expectancy theory (Vroom).

10 The *Critical Path Method* (CPM) is a project modelling technique developed in the late 1950s by Morgan R. Walker of DuPont and James E. Kelley, Jr. of Remington Rand and was developed for project management in the private sector. *Program Evaluation Review Technique* (PERT) is a similar methodology, a methodology developed by the US Navy in the 1950s to manage the Polaris submarine missile programme.

11 This is a paradox as art is collectable and a source of money but this issue will not be explored in the frame of this thesis.

12 Public Art Aberdeen is a website (http://www.aberdeencity.gov.uk/) created in 2011 dedicated to public art in Aberdeen. The site aspires to support production of new work in the city, break down barriers for communities, individuals, organisations, and businesses to become involved in public art, and to promote best practice. It developed a toolkit for commissioning public art showing methodologies of Project Management.

13 "The first difference between science and philosophy is their respective attitude toward chaos. Chaos is defined not so much by its disorder as by the infinite speed with which every form taking shape in it vanishes. It is a void that is not a noth-ingness but a *virtual,* containing all possible particles and drawing out all possible forms, which sprung up only to disappear immediately without consistency or reference, without consequence" (Deleuze and Guattari, 1994, p. 118).

14 In this research the idea of chaos theory was acknowledged in scientific disciplines as project management and in social sciences as cultural studies. Nevertheless, for the purposes of this research, it was chosen not to study chaos theory thoroughly.

3 Three multidisciplinarity projects combining art, cultural studies, and project management for social change

Intervene: Heroes and Villains: saving education

Intervene: Heroes and Villains is a multidisciplinary project addressing early-age school dropout using the disciplines of art, psychology, and social work. Cultural studies is seen as intrinsic to the project as the understanding and integration of existing cultural references was of great importance for the realisation and impact of the project. The limitations it shows in the knowledge of the professional use of project management and in the integration of existing cultural references are precisely what make it a case study for research in linking art, cultural studies, and project management in a multidisciplinary approach as an engine for achieving social change.

Developed in Lisbon, Portugal, between 2006 and 2007, *Intervene: Heroes and Villains* was designed for young students at risk of early school dropout, from the neighbourhood of Zambujal, in Amadora, a city very near to Lisbon. In the context of the Open Museum programme[1] developed by the Arts Education Department of the CAM (Modern Art Centre – Gulbenkian Foundation)[2] a partnership was established with the Attended Itineraries programme of the CESIS (Centre for Research in Social Intervention). Both institutions have shown, in their history and activities, a concern for social accountability.

The problem of early dropout from school and repetition at the elementary level was identified by CESIS as a heavy burden on the Portuguese suburban and poor areas as with the neighbourhood of Zambujal, in Amadora. This is a problem that dates back to the 1970s, when the first wave of migrants built the neighbourhood, and was associated with other problems such as unemployment, poverty, social exclusion, and minor crimes. The schools in this neighbourhood do not look into the specificities of the community, characterised by a strong presence of migrants and children of migrants who do not speak Portuguese (Silva, 2003). The young people of the second generation of migrants in the neighbourhood are raised in the streets, alone, with friends of the same age and siblings while their parents work several hours a day (CMA, 2008).[3] This is one of the reasons indicated by the team of *Intervene: Heroes and Villains* for the early-age school dropout and related consequences.

Based on the observation of the historical and cultural contexts of the community, characterised by segregation, poverty, and social exclusion, the two institutions put together their different skills in an artistic and social intervention project for the duration of a school year. The project acknowledged its limitations of intervention within a small part of the community (one class of one school, with a total of 13 students) to represent young people at the risk of early-age school dropout.

The project started off with a team composed of art historians, artists, and social workers. After the setting up, the team grew with psychologists, filmmakers, visual arts teachers, and museum educators. The decision of layering various artistic forms and other disciplines in a multidisciplinary team was taken at the early stages of the project. This was a natural choice as the pedagogical department of the CAM is based on the idea of multidisciplinarity and interrelatedness. A multidisciplinary team encompassing experts from social sciences and humanities (architects, artists, art historians) but also from exact sciences (mathematicians and physics), leads guided tours, workshops, and all art activities at the CAM.

The theme "Heroes and Villains" was proposed by the museum educators and negotiated with the young participants in a partnership process, having in mind the importance of empowering them. The theme explored notions of self, making the participants reflect on themselves as individuals looking at their strong and weak points and what they could do to change themselves. This theme was chosen following a careful analysis of the historical and cultural context of the community.

The project is characterised by strong participation of the young people at all stages, with a focus on decision-making which was relevant in terms of empowerment in this community as the participants felt how important they were for the project – in fact, they formed the identity of the project. The self-perception of the participants changed during the project: at the beginning of the project, to be a villain meant, to the young participants, to be powerful; in the process of reflecting on notions of self and the dichotomy villain–hero, to be a villain became seen as the option of the weak. The goal became then to be a hero with the power to change the world we live in (Susana Gomes da Silva, personal communication, 2012).

The group of young people of the neighbourhood of Zambujal made weekly visits to CAM, where they were introduced to artworks in various conceptual frameworks. It was not always easy to make the 13 young people go to CAM, which is located in the city centre, as this meant about one hour on public transport. Therefore, the pedagogical department of CAM initiated a routine of visits to the neighbourhood in Amadora. This shows good ability of adaptation to problems from the team but it also reveals a first poor understanding of the needs and will of this group.

The project leaders assumed that, if the early school dropout was solved, the other problems of the neighbourhood would be also, at least partially, solved. This assumption was due to the cultural, social, and historical contexts of the neighbourhood where the problem of early school dropout was identified.

Currently, the neighbourhood of Zambujal, in Amadora, is largely composed of social housing built by the IGAPHE (Instituto de Gestão e Alienação do Património Habitacional do Estado (Institute for the Management and Disposal of State Housing) during the 1970s. It has been subject to a programme of rehabilitation, developed in a partnership between the City Council of Amadora and IGAPHE.

The city of Amadora is located in the metropolitan area of the Portuguese capital, Lisbon and has 175,872 inhabitants, according to data of the Amadora City Council (2001). It was the first municipality to be built after the Portuguese revolution of the 25th April, in 1974. Between the 1950s and 1970s, there was a growth in population from people coming from Africa (in particular, Cape Verde) but also from rural areas of Portugal such as Alentejo and Beiras. Part of this growth provoked the start of clandestine neighbourhoods such as Cova da Moura, near the neighbourhood of Zambujal. The common denominator in these communities is poverty and cultural uprooting (CMA, 2008).[4] Poverty might not be an impediment to personal development but, without social integration, poverty can be very hard to overcome as observed in the neighbourhoods of Amadora, including Zambujal.

In 1974, the first wave of migrants arrived from the ex-Portuguese colonies in Africa. They clandestinely took the lands by the military road and built neighbourhoods characterised by small houses, bonded to each other, without water or light and built in a labyrinth of narrow roads 1 meter wide. Both the government and the City Council overlooked this unbridled construction, claiming to have no means to help these people's integration into Portuguese society and culture. These migrants did not speak Portuguese but only Creole and were received in Portugal as cheap labour working mainly in cleaning and construction. Today, four decades later, their children and grandchildren still struggle to be integrated in their own country, causing problems of identity.

Schools were the first institutions to contribute to disintegration, as they did not hold programmes to teach Portuguese for foreigners. In the years following the Portuguese revolution against 40 years' dictatorship, the Portuguese capital, Lisbon, needed cheap labour for construction of public and private enterprises. Such need was based on the assumption that construction is a translation for the development of a country, a tradition that goes back to the Portuguese discoveries of the 15th and 16th centuries. Against this backdrop, it was common to see teachers segregating their students in the classrooms. Morais (n.d) describes a story of a teacher in a school in Amadora who would not make any effort to teach the children from Cape Verde who would only speak in Creole. They would sit in the last row of the class, without understanding a word, sitting as far as possible from their peers and also from Portuguese culture. Many of these children never made it to second grade.

People connected to the defence of the migrants, including intellectuals from Cape Verde and religious institutions, joined forces to form associations to help teach Portuguese in the neighbourhood in the late 1970s and 1980s but it remains a problem today. There are still remnants from this recent history, especially in terms of segregation and social exclusion: even when the children speak Portuguese, they are still perceived by others and themselves as a social and cultural minority.

In a 2007 study made by the IDT (Instituto da Droga e Toxicodependência/Drugs and Drug Addiction Institute) the problems identified in the neighbourhood of Zambujal were mainly health- and social-related including: lack of structures for healthcare; pregnancy at early age; high-risk sexual behaviours; problems related to the consumption of drugs and alcohol; low level of academic education; early dropout age at school; unemployment; housing problems; and problems of integration within the ethnic minorities.

These problems, which are no different to the problems identified in the 1970s, were the ones identified as related to the problem of early school dropout. The aim of the project was to fight early school dropout through empowerment of the children/young adults. The project's wish was to directly engage these young people and surrounding community in producing, experiencing, mediating, creating, enjoying, and valuing arts and culture in its potential to act in the problem of early-age school dropout. Rather than developing activities for the community, the project developed a series of activities with the community, asking for active participation and engagement as well as co-creation. The assumption was that, by solving the problem of early school dropout, other problems in the community would also cease. It was a very well-intentioned departure point but it proved to be too ambitious for the time frame and resources.

Over nine months, the project developed with a multidisciplinary team of psychologists, social workers, visual art teachers, art historians, artists, filmmakers, and museum educators. Susana Gomes da Silva, director of the pedagogical department at CAM who was regarded as and called herself project manager, led the team. In a first reading, the project is successful as it shows very good visual and final formal results (a film documentary showing a multiplicity of stories told by the participants and an exhibition) and encompasses a multidisciplinary team, which was able to communicate successfully in the context of a so-called problematic community. On deeper inspection, however, the project showed problems in terms of planning and could not fully meet the high expectations in the long term. In other words, the results and impact were not sustainable.

Relations between the disciplines applied in this project seemed to be thought of logically as interdependence and complementarity. Formally, the project evolved in three artistic areas – theatre, photography, and video – as a means of promoting a critical and creative reflection around the idea of construction of the self. This is mindful of the idea of art as social system from the perspective of Marcuse's concept of art as a tool to perceive the world and ourselves. To Marcuse, the advantage of perception lies in the power to show society as it could be (rather than as it is, in Luhmann) and, in this way, change the idea we might have of it (1978). In this case, the belief of the project is that, through art it is possible to change self-perception showing how the participants could be as a means of influencing future behaviour and attitudes.

The rationale for this project also follows Bourdieu's perspective under which aesthetic codes are the attitudes and dispositions of their social actors. To Bourdieu, sociology should go beyond the scope of the individual actors' self-perception and understand the consequences each action has. The project relies on the belief that through self-perception, there will be consequences to the actions of each individual and these actions will ultimately have consequences to the group. However, in this case, the aim of stopping early-age school dropout in that community proved to be too ambitious. The project did have an impact in the participants but in the following years, the same problem remained across the community.

The project was based on practical work, developing from direct contact with the artworks of the collections and the temporary exhibitions at CAM. Starting off as the main aim, other objectives were set including: to promote the development of competencies in the use of arts (dramatic expression, photography, and video) as privileged media of learning; to give the young people creative tools to build new relations with their social and cultural surroundings and with which to perceive themselves and to promote a reflexive capacity in the cultural identity and meaning of hero and villain.

In this neighbourhood of Amadora, the power lies with the villain who controls the area through criminal activities that bring not only money but also fear associated with respect. Through the visual representations and links to fictional and well-known stories of heroes and villains, putting the focus on who could, in fact, have the power to change for the better in the long term, the teenagers began to change their reflections, their self-perception, and will to develop. These reflections were visually translated in the works developed by the participants where they made photographic self-portraits with keywords and small texts showing their goals for the future. Through a series of group activities and workshops the project created moments of debate and reflection about solving conflicts using techniques such as creative writing, paper games, and the *Theatre of the Oppressed*.

Recognising that humans have a unique ability to take action in the world while simultaneously observing themselves in action, Boal's *Theatre of the Oppressed* was based on the belief that the human was a self-contained theatre, actor, and spectator in one. Because we can observe ourselves in action, we can amend, adjust, and alter our actions to have a different impact and to change our world (Boal, 1992). This concept is mindful of the idea of social sculpture coined by artist Joseph Beuys, which claimed that every individual could be an artist. Both concepts imply empowerment through participation and social engagement – only with the participation of the audience/citizens can the work come to fruition and meet its purpose of social transformation.

The application of participatory methodologies in decision-making during the project resulted in outcomes such as a video documentary and a series of staged photographic self-portraits, which proved very important in changing the self-perception of the young participants. The methodologies became an engine for achieving self-confidence, which was shown in the participants' efforts to become someone who could not only change individually (which in this case would be converted into not dropping out of school) but also contribute to producing effective change in their neighbourhood.

Even though this change of self-perception is a successful outcome, it only occurred in the participants of the project, which lead to a short-term impact despite the high expectations of future developments, possibly due to, on one hand, a lack of a deep study of the cultural references of the community and, on the other hand, of the roots of the education problem encountered. The very fact that children dropout from school in large numbers and at an early age leads back to the fundamental questions of what meaning education has or what role it plays in different social settings. Some of the questions posed by the project included: Why should families make an effort to keep their children in school at all? What is the importance of education in their lives? And how does going to school, the educational project, fit together with other, perhaps more urgent, things to do in life? This leads to a number of other basic questions. In order to understand the significance of education for different social groups (in this case, with the specificity of the Zambujal neighbourhood which was mentioned in the previous section), we must know something about the capacity of these groups to make use of the education system. What, then, are the economic, social, and cultural resources that different families or social groups have at their disposal when they try to make use of school? Economic resources include such things as having money to pay for schooling (school fees, textbooks, clothes, in urban areas nowadays also bribes, etc.) and being able to do without the labour force of children during the time used for school. Social resources seem to be related to such things as having useful contacts (for example, close relatives in town when children have nowhere to go when parents are working and classes finish), or not being subject to social prejudice when belonging to a cultural minority.

Cultural resources also seem to mean, in a general and arguable point of view, the kind of cultural competence a family can have that normally only comes with formal education, such as being able to read and write or knowing what goes on in school and in the education system. Admittedly, these are very general questions and attempting to answer them would imply an enormous amount of research; it seems that the research involved in the project missed understanding the cultural references in relation to what these might mean in the present and, essentially, in a possible future of the neighbourhood with its historical, social, and economic context. This lack of understanding seemed to affect the success of the project since it had many expectations for the future of the neighbourhood and it ended with helping to solve the early age of school dropout in that academic year, which is a short-term goal far from the initial aim of changing the reality of the neighbourhood in terms of prejudice, poverty, and other issues that the project leaders thought could be solved through resolving early-age dropout.

Ideas of project management were applied during the project but not as thoroughly and deeply as its professional meaning. The concept of project manager was mentioned several times in interviews conducted during this research but as a loose notion. According to Weaver, the employment of people as project managers only started to emerge in the 20th century. Before that, the leadership of the project venture existed between the generalist role held by the coordinating architects, who were responsible for every single aspect of strategy and delivery including cost control and time management, and the specialist roles and responsibilities allocated by the concept of contract in the 18th and 19th centuries to the concepts of programme and then project management in the 20th century (Wæver, 2007). In *Intervene: Heroes and Villains*, the idea of project manager is precisely that of a generalist role of leadership and coordination described by Weaver.

In terms of application of methodologies of project management observed in *Intervene: Heroes and Villains*, the project claims to have followed five phases. According to the Project Management Body of Knowledge (PMBOK; PMI, 1996), the process of directing and controlling a project from start to finish may be further divided into five basic phases, the same that were followed during the nine months of *Intervene: Heroes and Villains*. The five phases were well documented in the project, which is remarkable as there were no professional project managers assigned in the team, even though the names given to each phase were different from those coined by the Project Management Institute (PMI) and described in Figure 3.1. The project leader of *Intervene: Heroes and Villains*, Susana Gomes da Silva, described the descriptions of each phase.

a. Project concept/idea (in the project the first phase was named Initiation)

The idea for the project was carefully examined to determine whether and how it would benefit the community of young people at risk of early-age school dropout. Statistical data available in the City Councils of Lisbon and Amadora were analysed in order to construct an overall picture of dropout and repetition. Later, during the research, data from the specific neighbourhood of Zambujal and even particular schools were re-analysed for the specific purpose of selecting one class from one school. One of the selection criteria was interest in participating. The poor response to this criterion was one of the problems faced by the project's team. Even though there was

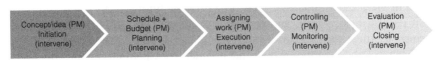

Figure 3.1 The phases of a project in the light of project management and in the light of *Intervene: Heroes and Villains*

concern that the project could work in the short term but fail in the long term – the students involved could benefit in the year of the project but the impact on their futures and in other classes and schools in the same neighbourhood were very uncertain – the team decided to pursue the project. During this phase, the decision-making was shared between the team leader and team members and it was concluded that the project could realistically be completed in the set time frame. Following this conclusion, the negotiation of the theme with the young participants began.

b. Project schedule and budget (in the project the second phase was named Planning)

A project plan and a project charter were set to outline the work to be performed. During this phase, the team leader calculated a budget and schedule for the nine months of the project duration and determined what human resources as well as practical tools were needed. A deeper evaluation of the cultural and social context of the neighbourhood of Zambujal took place at this stage, with interviews of students, teachers, and parents, and regular visits to the neighbourhood conducted by the project team members. Over nine months, the project included 75 hours of workshops and 120 hours of preparation and planning.

c. Assigning the work to team members (in the project the third phase was named Execution)

During this phase, resources and tasks were distributed and team members were informed of responsibilities such as: visiting the neighbourhood of Zambujal, meeting with the young people at risk of early dropout from school, meeting with the parents and teachers of the young people to evaluate progress in terms of attendance of school classes, leading the workshops, and art directing the film documentary and the staged photographic portraits (the two outputs of the project). During the Execution phase, described by the project leader as the phase of "Assigning the work to team members" (Susana Gomes da Silva, personal communication, 2012), important project-related information (such as the cultural and social context of the neighbourhood and the importance of empowerment to this community through the dichotomy heroes–villains) was brought up.

d. Controlling project status (in the project the fourth phase was named Monitoring)

Project leader Susana Gomes da Silva compared project status and progress to the actual plan, as team members and participants performed the scheduled work. The schedule needed various adjustments in terms of phases and activities, but the project followed the initial duration plan of nine months.

e. Evaluation (in the project the fifth phase was named Closing)

The evaluation was made in a continuous and participative methodology, framed by the aims of the project, including a film documentary, which is a creative solution to present a report that can otherwise fall into the trap of being very difficult to read with figures and numbers rather than a story.

In this evaluation process, it was crucial to meet regularly within the project team as well as with the young participants (Susana Gomes da Silva, personal communication, 2012). The three management meetings contemplated a moment of audit and evaluation for the team leaders. The working sessions were planned with a methodology that would permit moments of evaluation from the young participants in order to promote responsibility in all participants in terms of decision-making. The evaluation of the young participants allowed planning of all sessions adequate to the needs of the community. There was also a follow-up in the subsequent academic year with the students and it was verified that all participants were studying with good grades. In terms of the goals of the project, it was partially successful as it did benefit part of the community of young people at risk of early-age school dropout and a change in terms of perception of the importance of school by the parents and friends of the young participants was also observed. It is expected that this project will lead on to further projects and initiatives that will promote the importance of studies in this community (Susana Gomes da Silva, personal correspondence, 2013) but no plans are made to promote or encourage such activities.

Even though the project succeeded in preventing school dropout in the students with whom they worked, the project did not succeed in changing that reality as it seems not to have had an effect on the other students as the problem of early-age dropout remains in that community as stated by Susana Gomes da Silva in an interview.

Evaluation is key in projects as it allows for a clear understanding of what has worked and what has not. Main goals of evaluation include measuring possible long-term results; outlining "lessons learned" during the implementation; formulating recommendations for similar actions in the future; and making recommendations to stakeholders (participants but also other schools and local organisations in this and in similar neighbourhoods) dealing with segregation. In the case of *Intervene: Heroes and Villains,* the evaluation was continuous which allowed issues such as the difficulty of taking participants to the museum to be corrected, but did not measure the impact of the project, which would be fundamental for future activities.

Project Row Houses: all artists are alike

Initiated by artist, architect, and community activist Rick Lowe in 1993, *Project Row Houses* is an ongoing project that aims to stimulate and create alternative methods of development in art, culture, and economics in

Houston's Third Ward, one of the city's oldest African-American communities. The sound knowledge of the project's team in the history and culture of the community is rather unique and the main reason for its selection as a case study in this research.

Project Row Houses began when Lowe discovered the abandoned one and a half block site of 22 shotgun-style houses that were, at the time, marked for demolition. The Third Ward's neighbourhood was then characterised by, on one hand, a housing problem (a large number of rundown and abandoned houses) and, on the other hand, a lack of viable private enterprises which resulted in a high unemployment rate with its associated problems including poverty, crime, deteriorating housing, and poor health care for the community's citizens.

The Third Ward is a neighbourhood in Houston that was historically populated by African Americans. By the 1880s, approximately 25% of black households in Third Ward were owner-occupied. The homes built in the Third Ward followed a number of vernacular styles, including some that were hybrids – an innovation brought about by the advent of house catalogues, which allowed homeowners to pick the style of house they wanted to build and add on details from other styles listed.

This resulted in the diffusion of regional styles on a national level, including one commonly found in Houston's black communities: the shotgun house. Given this name because a shotgun shell fired at the front door would travel through the house and out the back door without hitting anything, shotgun

Figure 3.2 Project Row Houses, 2009
Source: Photograph by Hourick. Creative Commons Attribution 3.0 Unported license

houses were one room wide, one story tall, with the rooms arranged in a row without hallways, and doors at opposite ends of the facade. Though some relate the style to the New York brownstone, the shotgun is believed to have travelled from New Orleans, where such houses date back to about 1800. Others believe it originated in West African house building traditions, or that the shotgun represents a New World Euro-American hybrid style that came to New Orleans via Haiti (Vlach, 1976). Even when transformed over the years by others, the shotgun house expresses the enduring social values and cultural traditions of African Americans. For newly freed African Americans, the shotgun was not only a symbol of freedom but also a means of defining themselves as a united community outside the confines of slavery.

The shotgun form grew out of the value traditional African society placed on the continuity of the extended family and a reverence for one's ancestors. In its history, the shotgun house has often been raised as a contemporaneous witness to the struggle of a people for dignity and a place in the American social, economic, and cultural panorama. Despite its relevance as a witness to a people's history, the shotgun house has not harvested quite the same degree of mainstream recognition and respect as such other historically rooted African-American cultural forms like music, literature, and dance (Upton and Vlach, 1986).

In America, many seem to falsely assume that shotgun houses are nothing more than architectural extensions of the slave cabin. Many understand the shotgun house as a neo-slave cabin, because of the persistent degradation of blacks during the zenith of shotgun construction.

With four million former slaves seeking low-cost housing, from the Reconstruction times to the 1920s, untold scores of shotgun homes were built, making it the primary and most prevalent housing type in America during that time. In order to meet the housing needs spawned by the Great Migration, mail order plans and construction materials for shotgun homes were broadly available by 1900, making it both popular and economical to build in urban as well as rural settings. By the 1930s, the shotgun represented 60% to more than 80% of the housing stock for African Americans in a considerable number of Southern communities (Kniffen, 1936). While the vernacular style initially represented a source of self-esteem for African Americans, it later acquired the stigma of stereotypical perceptions (Entman, 1990). It was the identification of these perceptions and what it meant to the community of the Third War (such as unemployment and poverty) that inspired the existence of *Project Row Houses*. The project looked thoroughly into the true history as well as small stories of the Third Ward and its type of architecture to establish its goals and actions.

After studying the architecture of the houses and their history in social and cultural terms, which reflected diverse self-contained African-American communities, Lowe decided to start a refurbishing process in a new form of artistic, cultural, and social action among the community. Lowe assumed that these houses could provide both a powerful and accessible material link to the African-American past and a setting within which the work of contemporary

African-American artists could be produced and accessible to the African-American community of the Third Ward.

Based on this assumption, the houses were transformed into affordable homes for single mothers and artists-in-residence, while maintaining their architectural integrity. Locating the shotgun houses as a focal point of the Third Ward, Lowe has rewritten the traditional narrative of urban redevelopment – the houses became, rather than a visual translation of poverty and crime, an element to be celebrated and linked to cultural traditions.

Since its inception, *Project Row Houses* has grown both in spatial and programmatic terms: from the original one and a half to six blocks, and from 22 to 40 houses, which include 12 exhibition and artist-in-residency spaces, seven houses for young mothers (Young Mothers Residential Programme providing housing and counselling on personal growth and parenting skills), office spaces, a community gallery, a park, and a series of low-income residential and commercial spaces. *Project Row Houses* can be described today as a project based on "art and cultural education, historic preservation, neighbourhood revitalization and community service" (Tucker, 1995).

In 2003, *Project Row Houses* established the Row House Community Development Corporation as a separate corporation. It was created with the aim of broadening the project's focus to preserve community and addresses housing and related community and economic development needs by providing low-income rental housing.

In 2012, Project Row Houses was in the mist of developing its 10-year plan. The plan had two parts: local, and national and international activities. At local level, the plan was described as a "continuation of growing impact within the 40-block area by building additional houses, preserving architecture, both houses and commercial buildings, adding new cultural and social service facilities, and nurturing small business development." At national and international level, Project Row Houses defined their methodology and, in 2012, began a process of selecting sites to expand the project in similar social and cultural contexts (Lowe, 2012).

Project Row Houses exists comfortably between the worlds of different disciplines:

> The multi-layering of the different ways of seeing, i.e., artists, architects, community members, historians, arts administrators, developers, etc., gave the project a complexity that was more natural than if it was developed strictly by artists or architects. If it was not for the multiple interests in the project, I'm not sure if it would have been sustainable or on going. It's expected for artists or architects to think about the "final" product of their work, but when community interest, i.e., residents, city government, historian, administrators, etc., are truly connected to the project, the vitality of the project becomes creatively responding to the issues and challenges brought forth by the community. Not in the refinement of the final product.
>
> (Lowe, 2012)

Rick Lowe started the project in 1993 having in mind the artistic, cultural, and economic development of the Third Ward. His idea to create temporary public art installations in the Third Ward's neighbourhood grew out of discussions about how African-Americans in Houston could make their work more accessible to the African-American community.

Rick Lowe is highly influenced by Beuys's concept of social sculpture and by artist John Biggers (1924–2001), who was born in a shotgun house. *Project Row Houses* is founded on the principle that art creates a community, in a social activity, and that can be the foundation for revitalising depressed inner-city neighbourhoods. In this way, *Project Row Houses* can be compared to the idea of social sculpture or sculpture as an art form and a social activity where every individual can be an artist in the sense that all citizens are capable of transforming (parts of) society – in this case, to change the poverty scenario of the Third Ward.

At a symbolic level, *Project Row Houses'* programmes are a translation of the work of artist John Biggers, in which the shotgun house is a recurring symbol of the African-American cultural landscape. The project decodes the artist's principles concerning the components of row house communities: art and creativity; education; social safety nets; architecture; and sustainability.

The programmes and activities at *Project Row Houses* advocate that art and creativity should be viewed as an integral part of life, exemplified in African cultural traditions wherein art is interwoven into the very fabric of life through rituals and ceremonial activities, an idea that resonates with Beuys's concept of social sculpture. Through artists, the project provides opportunities to identify problems. Then, through the organisation of the project, creative solutions are sought such as the Young Mothers Programme designed for low-income, young mothers between the ages of 18 and 26 who envision success in spite of their circumstances. In this way, the community and its residents become form and content for artists and the organisation. For many of the artists who work in the Third Ward community, this is one of their primary focuses and if the culture of the community becomes integral to the work, the artists or their artistic approaches also become integral to the community in addressing problems (Lowe, 2012).

Project Row Houses' central mission is to establish a forum for dialogue between artists and the Third Ward community within the context of its African-American culture and history. During a residency, an artist is required to conduct workshops with community members where they discuss their installations in the houses or give instructions for small art projects. The work produced and exhibited within these characteristics of participation and collaboration express a framework of cultural self-definition and collective identity which is inherently bound up with the traditions, history, and social values of the African-American community. The project challenges each artist to interweave his personal vision with the community and the unique space of the shotgun house – echoing the traditional African artisan's creative process of melding collective values and personal visions (Willett, 1971).

Project Row Houses was initiated with long-term goals and strategies were applied, at an informal level, from the very start with contributions from professional art managers, administrators, community members, historians, and developers. The strategies of project management identified in Project Row Houses share a common preoccupation with routine, day-to-day maintenance of the work processes and people for whom they are responsible. The idea of project in *Project Row Houses* is closer to the definition presented in "PMBOK – A guide to the Project Management Body Of Knowledge" – "a temporary endeavour undertaken to create a unique product, service or result" – than to Alan Stretton's conceptualisation: "project management or at least the profession and practice of modern project management as it is embodied in the various project management associations around the world" (Stretton, 1994). Project management as described by organisations such as the APMi (UK) and PMIii in their respective bodies of knowledge (BoKs) are not applied in *Project Row Houses*. The core of their processes is not implemented by the consistent use of templates, forms, and software, and the overall methodology is not supported and developed by some form of project management office (PMO). In *Project Row Houses*, the leadership of the project endeavour spans from a generalist role for all aspects of design and delivery including cost control and time management to responsibility for identifying stakeholders, presenting a strategy, and raising funds. Furthermore, it did not follow the five stages of project management observed in *Intervene: Heroes and Villains*.

Even though their approach could be better identified with an early concept of project management, *Project Row Houses* is successfully managed. In the same year it was initiated, the Project has been incorporated as a non-profit organisation, obtained a five-year, lease-purchase agreement for the site and was awarded in grants from local and national arts foundations. Lowe, who supplemented his artist's income with carpentry work, began renovating the first house himself with the goal of opening the project to the public within the year.

Lowe had originally intended to acquire only ten of the site's houses and use them as art installation spaces, but it became clear that much more funding from foundation and government sources would be available for housing than for galleries. A low-income housing component would provide ongoing income to keep the galleries open, and by acquiring all the houses on the site, the project could control the ensemble of buildings and spaces, which was one of the aims.

In their first steps, *Project Row Houses* assumed that art alone could produce change in terms of perception. This was, partially, correct as once the neighbourhood looked cleaner and nicer in aesthetical terms, it became more attractive to visitors who, gradually, stopped being afraid of passing by and going there. This change, however, did not translate to better financial conditions. When asked directly what they thought of the changes made by the artists, the people living there mentioned it looked nice but what they really needed were jobs:

> Through our formal programmes, there are a number of things we have identified that drives our work. One thing that we have noticed is that because of economic conditions in our community, most of the people we work with do not have the ability or interest in looking at education in the abstract.
>
> (Lowe, 2012)

In the following steps, the project's members worked on this and found ways to help the community to create their own jobs. As an example, Lowe and his team coached one man who used to make barbecues in his family parties to turn this into a small business run from his own home. This included support for communication and management in the implementation of his small business.

Lowe and co-director Deborah Grotfeld assembled a multidisciplinary team of community members, social workers, artists, and architects to apply for a HUD grant (US Department of Housing and Urban Development grant)[5] that would provide the financial resources to restore the site but the application was unsuccessful. Despite the final result, the process of application led to the development of a plan which included all the houses on the site, with seven transitional houses for low-income families and five houses for community service projects. One house would become the Spoken Word House, dedicated to poetry readings and writers' workshops.

In this plan, the adjacent two-story storefront, an integral part of the site, would serve as an ideal landmark for the project as a multimedia performing arts centre. The centre would be programmed in relation to the artists' installations and provide income for the project. An open space where five houses had been demolished would be developed as a community sculpture and vegetable garden and would visually unite the houses and the two-story storefront.

With foundation grants and favourable media reports in hand, Lowe and Grotfeld quickly found local stakeholders such as corporations, local museums, community churches, and individual donors to sponsor the concretisation of this plan. The exterior of the houses was then restored to their original appearance in accordance with Texas Historical Commission guidelines, but the interior finish was left up to the individual artists, who transformed the space with each installation.

The project has guaranteed its sustainability over time and with five to ten years' planning involving local public and private organisations in decision-making. Such method has proved that through lasting relationships of trust, collaboration, and participation, projects become collective endeavours where each part/individual brings his/her own resources that can be financial but also knowledge and expertise.

Today, more than 20 years after its implementation, *Project Row Houses* presents itself as a "community-based arts and culture non-profit organisation," which "shifts the view of art from traditional studio practice to a more conceptual base of transforming the social environment." The project not only helped community members in creating jobs, it also created job opportunities within the organisation. Furthermore, *Project Row Houses* has also managed to sustain its artistic programme based on Biggers principles (public art; education; social safety nets; sustainability; and architecture) with the support of sponsors such as The Brown Foundation; Bruner Foundation Inc.; Chevron; Houston Endowment Inc.; Joan Hohlt and Roger Wich Foundation; The Kinder Foundation; The Kresge Foundation; The Lewis Family Foundation; Marc Melcher; John P. McGovern Foundation; National Endowment for the Arts; Nightingale Code Foundation; Betty Pecore and Howard Hilliard; Picnic; Robert Rauschenberg Foundation; The Simmons Foundation Inc.; Surdna Foundation; Texas Commission on the Arts; Susan Vaughan Foundation; and a grant from the City of Houston through Houston Arts Alliance. The path of the project, with its multiple narratives, shows that there are alternative ways of successfully managing a project.

Morrinho: making a (not so) small revolution

Morrinho is a project that started in a Brazilian favela as a children's game, by children and for children. It evolved to become regarded as an artwork and, eventually, it developed into an NGO fighting the preconceived ideas of the reality of favelas. Due to the many narratives and alternative narratives at cultural and disciplinary levels that *Morrinho* presupposes, it was important to analyse it in depth.

Morrinho is a social and cultural project based out of the Pereira da Silva favela, which shares its location with the wealthy southern zone of Rio de Janeiro. Nelcirlan Souza de Oliveira, a 14-year-old boy who had recently moved to Rio de Janeiro, created *Morrinho*, the project further studied in this section, in 1997, without a specific aim besides playing. It then evolved into an artistic project and today it is an NGO aiming at social change. The people living in favelas, maybe due to the lack of resources, possess a "do-it-yourself" spirit and a "build-your-own" mentality. These were the founding characteristics of *Morrinho*, with its aim of changing the dogmatic perception of the favelas. The project addresses and questions the well-accepted attitude of assigning to the urban poor responsibility for their alleged lack of integration into the city's culture and immediate associations with poverty, crime, and drugs.

The reality of *the* favela arrives in our homes via the media in rough images of crime, drug abuse, conflict, and violence that make up a unified image of what favelas are. The reality that *Morrinho* shows of Pereirão, however, is based on various small stories of one favela that contradict the grand narrative of the favela as a unified entity.

Figure 3.3 Morrinho, 2009
Source: Photograph by Austin Jabari Freeman. Creative Commons Attribution –
ShareAlike 3.0 License

The grand narrative of the favela

In current discourse, when one says the word favela, commonly, the associations made are with social problems, segregation, and urban violence. A historical reading shows however that the favela has been a topic of debate for at least a century, concurrent with a chain of images and representations that diverges from the social constructions that politicians, writers, and social scientists have built up over the years in dealing with this particular social and urban phenomenon (Valladares, 2009). Looking at the origin of the word favela, it was first cited in 19th-century Portuguese dictionaries, and it meant favela tree, which was commonly found in Bahia.

After the Guerra de Canudos (Canudos War) in Bahia, between 1895 and 1896, government soldiers, who had lived amongst favela trees,[6] trailed to Rio de Janeiro to get their expected payment for war service. They settled on one of Rio's hills and gave it the name "Morro da Favela" because of the tree that prospered in the location of their victory against the rebels of the Canudos War. They waited for their payment but it never came, so they decided not to leave the Morro da Favela, which became the first favela in history.

The development of the idea of what a favela might represent, in terms of popular and academic writing, started at the beginning of the 20th century. Many descriptions of the favela in the first half of the 20th century appeared

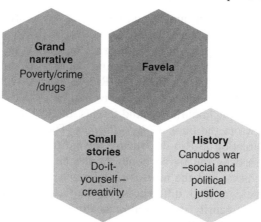

Figure 3.4 The layers of the favela: grand narrative; small stories; history

in the form of journalistic or historical writing. Euclides da Cunha's well-known book *Os Sertões* (1902) covers the Canudos War and describes the coast versus the back lands as the opposition between cultured and uncultured, making a comparison to explain the difference between the favela and the city. The history of the favelas is thus one of land invasion by poverty-stricken migrants, impoverished soldiers.

In essays by architects, social workers, and doctors that entered the communities at the beginning of the 20th century, the favela was described as wrong, poor and dirty. This period was highly significant because it created the image of favela as the habitat of the poor (Perlman, 1977), an idea that still prevails in popular representations and people's minds during the 20th and 21st century.

In the 1940s, a housing crisis characterised by the high prices of houses and the law of supply and demand forced people with low income, mainly migrants, to build illegal houses in the Federal District. This crisis was mainly due to Getúlio Vargas's industrialisation. The constructions were in morros (hills), vertically instead of horizontally due to the lack of space for more construction as well as the topography of the hills. Favelas became the main type of residence for cariocas (residents of Rio de Janeiro) in contrast to legally-built apartments.

The 1960s present an exponential increase in the number of publications about favelas. This decade can be described as the moment in which the favela becomes an academic research subject internationally. In the same decade, favelas expanded into the metropolitan periphery of Rio. Most of the existent favelas today began in the 1970s, as a result of a construction boom, initiated by a rural exodus of workers from poorer states in Brazil, in the more prosperous districts of Rio de Janeiro.

The population of Rio de Janeiro is about 6,150,000 (as of 2004), occupying an area of 1,256 km^2. The larger metropolitan area population is estimated at 10–13 million, and a quarter of the city is living in hundreds of favela communities. The percentage of favelas in Brazil is 36.6% (UN-HABITAT, 2003). This percentage is not particular to Brazil only as favelas (named differently in different countries and cultures as stated before) are rising globally. Despite the attempts that Rio de Janeiro is making to integrate these informal communities into the formal city, there is still a big gap between traditional neighbourhoods and favelas. In 1994, Brazilian journalist Zuenir Ventura wrote the book *Cidade Partida* (The Divided City), clearly portraying the situation in Rio de Janeiro: the enormous social gap between what are described as the paved zones of the city, with asphalted roads and spectacular bays, and the morros or hills, where most of Rio's favelas are located. These critical differences have to do with access to basic municipal services, security issues, public health, employment opportunities, and perception that affect those living in favelas.

As Brazil's civil society expanded, growing attention and research on the favela, both from academics and politicians, led to NGOs increasingly entering these communities, setting up programmes and doing their own research, adding to the growing body of literature and knowledge, as well as changing the perception of what a favela might really mean. In 2007, President Lula announced the Programa de Aceleração do Crescimento (Programme for Acceleration and Growth), a four-year investment plan, which included the promotion of urban development for the favelas. There have been public policies from local governments specially directed at the favelas. In Rio de Janeiro, programmes such as the Favela-Bairro[7] and Rio Cidade[8] have attempted to mitigate the problem of poverty and weak development within the favelas. The problem with these programmes is that the community does not make them or even participate in them. Instead, people living outside make these programmes, coming up with solutions to what they think might be the problems to solve. Usually, this leads to little participation and short-term change. In contrast, community-initiated programmes, as *Morrinho*, count with major participation.

The word on the streets and the national and international media are not helping change the dogmas and prejudices commonly held about the favela. The basic assumption remains unchanged: the favela is a space constructed by and for the urban poor, where drug dealing and crime grow. Forming an illegal city within the legal and normalised city, favelados[9] create a territory with a clearly marked identity. In this space, which is discarded by the public authorities, a parallel economy develops, with its own laws and rules. In this sense, the favela is the emblem of social segregation. The word favela is commonly associated with the word slum, shantytown, squatter community, or ghetto. Each of these words convey a negative undertone, slum suggests squalor, shantytown insinuates shaky housing, squatter community makes allusions to illegality, and ghetto assumes violence. These definitions are unfair and are far from the fullness of favela culture and the origin of favela in Bazilian history.

In order to truly change this perception of what a favela might mean, a first step would be, probably, to refer to its true form. It is true that there is crime and drugs in favelas, but it is also true, and rejected from media and common knowledge, that the definitions that represent the essence of a favela are straight, organised, solid communities, where conscientious people have spent decades empowering with barely a government service in sight.

Unfolding Morrinho's narratives

Changing the perception of what a favela might be is at the core of *Morrinho*. Their aim is to bring positive change to their local community, as well as challenge the popular perception of Brazil's favelas. The belief that favelas are merely dominated by drug trafficking and violence is not all-encompassing. In an interview published in the frame of the seminar "There is no knife without roses," Chico Serra and Cilan Oliveira tell how *Morrinho* started off as a children's game. As a 14-year-old boy, Oliveira was impressed with the architecture and style of life in the favela and he decided to playfully reproduce this reality in his own backyard with bricks and paint left over from his father's construction work. This diversion caught the attention of several other local children, and what was once just a game turned into their reality and routine. In a short time, a miniature favela of 350 square meters took shape (Serra and Oliveira, 2012).

Within the miniature urban world of *Morrinho*, they acted out a role-playing game with the numerous Lego-block avatars that inhabit the model, recreating life in this Rio's favela, with samba performances and gangs cohabiting in the same place. Currently, more than 20 teenagers are following the example of the founding members.

Interestingly, the project was never planned as a work of art but it was a very natural step to change itself from play to art, as with its amazing aesthetics and the ingenuity of its child creators, it attracted artists and filmmakers. In 2001, the encounter between filmmakers and producers Fábio Gavião and Marco Oliveira with the young creators of the model was crucial for what became *Morrinho*. The idea of Fábio Gavião and Marco Oliveira, when they climbed the hill of Pereira da Silva and first saw Morrinho was to create a collaborative documentary with the young people from the community. Even though the trust and empowerment elements were not tackled in the interviews, it seems that the fact that the filmmakers trusted these children in giving them expensive cameras, had an empowering effect as the children felt responsible for both the cameras and producing something worthy of the confidence that the filmmakers showed in them.

The recordings they produced turned into short films and were used in the documentary "Deus Sabe de Tudo Mas Não é X9" (God knows everything but is not a snitch). By giving the cameras to the children, and trusting them, the filmmakers contributed to the main aim of what became *Morrinho*: to change the negative perception of what a favela might be. This relates to

Luhmann's idea of art as a social system, in which art's role is based on the perception of the world as it is rather than what it could be. What *Morrinho* is hoping and aiming for is to change the common perception of favela – their observations are then subject to other observations when they show the documentary or the model of *Morrinho* outside the favela of Pereirão.

Robert Storr, curator and art critic who curated the Venice Biennale in 2007, got to know about Morrinho through the work of the artist and photographer Paula Trope, who presented a photographic exhibition in partnership with *Morrinho*'s artists at the São Paulo Biennial in 2006. Chico Serra says that Storr simply showed up in the community and said he wanted the young creators to reproduce a model of Morrinho at the Venice Biennale. Oliveira and Serra recount how meaningful this was to them then as young boys, as this allowed them to travel to Europe, something they could never have dreamed of before (Serra and Oliveira, 2012). But it is also interesting to look at the choice of Robert Storr as a curator. Since the nineties, as described in the previous chapter, there is a growing interest in social change and social practice within the arts and also within art institutions. There is a recent flow of contemporary artists entering the social realm, in projects that range from communicating ideas to asking for participation and, sometimes, taking political action (Lind, 2011). Following the interest of artists, art critics and art institutions have been writing essays and putting up exhibitions exploring the ideas of social practice and social sculpture. The difference between such projects and *Morrinho* is that the latter is done by and for the community whereas artist-initiated projects are made by outsiders assuming to know what a specific community needs and wants.

In the Venice Biennale's exhibition catalogue, Robert Storr compares *Morrinho* to Beuys's idea of social sculpture (Storr, 2007). It is a very interesting parallel, as the community as a whole can be regarded as one great work of art to which each young creator contributes creatively in a very horizontal and non-hierarchical way, without being influenced or knowing Beuys's idea of social sculpture. Creatively, this seems to be a plus but, in organisational terms, it can be difficult to make a plan and establish goals when all authors are involved in all decisions at all times, without a clear division of roles. Despite the difficulties encountered by not having a clear leadership style, they have managed, through a collaborative model that can, sometimes, be very chaotic and an engine for small conflicts between the members, to evolve and implement their activities.

Since its first appearance at the 2003 International Rio Architecture Exhibition at the Cultural Center of Parque das Ruínas in Rio de Janeiro to more recent shows such as the installation and video performance *TV Morrinho Live* at the Wiener Festwochen in Vienna (2008), Festival Brazil in London (2010), Convention Center in Dili (East Timor), and The Great Babylon Circus in the Netherlands (both in 2011), the aesthetics of *Morrinho* have been adapting to different local, spatial, and structural conditions, incorporating everyday objects and icons from the places through which it passes, creating new meanings – as well as levels of interpretation and appropriation – for these spaces.

Through a collaborative work process, from preparation of the bricks to painting the houses for the installation, reconstructing *Morrinho* also represents an eternal transformation in the lives of its creators, who are still living in a Rio de Janeiro favela and whose anarchic architecture surrounds them every day. *Morrinho* endures as an independent, artistic process, while also building a new organisation based on the cooperation of its artists–founders and collaborators. More than a reflection on the social geography that permeates Brazilian communities, *Morrinho* ponders a more harmonised relationship between the formal city and the favela, seeking other perceptions about the ethics and aesthetics of the slums.

External observers (as the Association of Inhabitants of Pereirão and the Hostel Favelinha) regard *Morrinho* as an organisation typical of Rio, despite its national and international reach. *Morrinho* shares and expresses the culture of the Carioca, the way it embraces edges and off-centre experiences and brings the marginal back to the centre of its identity (Lima, 1996; Velho and Alvito, 1996). The relations between the hill and the asphalt have always been emblematic of this dynamic, explored by Brazilian social scientists not only in relation to Rio but also to Brazil as a whole (Vianna, 2001). Drawing on these cultural practices, they treat difference, conflict, and tension as sources of transformation. They are explicitly inspired by Brazilian cultural movements (Ramos, 2007), which subvert logics of colonisation and exclusion by advocating mixture and the blending of extreme difference.

A culture of celebration and of artistic expression mixed with partying and entertainment is another element that characterises *Morrinho*, stemming from Brazilian culture, in particular from its black heritage. Despite the harshness and suffering of favela experiences, this group introduce the favela through films, music, and dance, breaking away from what is seen as an "angry," "annoyed," "moaning," style of putting forward an agenda of social change. They draw from the experience of slavery and survival in adversity and, in particular, from the lessons embedded in the use of music and bodily expression as forms of resistance, something that is clearly recognised by observers. By using and expressing cultural resources that reverberate across a wide range of partners and the diverse landscape of the city and of the country, *Morrinho*'s actions trigger cognitive and emotional solidarities both inside and outside favelas. They irradiate cultural codes across the city and beyond while at the same time pushing an agenda of citizenship, social justice, and urban equality.

A notable report named "Underground Sociabilities" (Jovchelovitch and Hérnandez, 2012) concluded that the work conducted by AfroReggae and Cufa[10] consists of an innovative social technology that can be adopted in other parts of the world. Professor Jovchelovitch, who directed the study, commented:

The efficacy of those organisations derives from the wisdom, culture and identity present at the communities they belong to and represent. Their projects fulfil multiple functions and offer lessons that must be heeded. The social capital of Brazil and the social development model found in Rio can be transferred – and hugely contribute – to improve life conditions of excluded populations all over the world.

(Jovchelovitch and Hérnandez, 2012)

The above-mentioned study observed that, in favelas, the family is central to socialisation, but so are grass-roots organisations, something that can be observed in *Morrinho* as well. Creators and new participants were brought up in the favelas of Rio, exposed to broken homes and to poverty, used to confrontation with the police and to the violence and loss caused by the drug trade. Most did not finish school, and those who did mention issues of access and quality of education. They tell personal histories where failure, loss, poverty, racism, and discrimination were frequently experienced. Contained in the narrative of the background are situations of desperation, of being "fallen," of being on the floor, situations that push them to the edge and produce intense personal crises. These include the loss of loved ones, being close to death and to entering the drug trade, and attempted suicide.

The children who initiated *Morrinho* were left alone most of the day, as their parents would go to their jobs, and they chose to play and build a model of a favela. Eventually, it became a work of art and, after, an NGO. As an NGO, *Morrinho* operates, in many ways, as parents by proxy. Mentoring people, offering them strong role models and emotional support alongside educational and training opportunities, is what ultimately allows rewriting of life stories, as some of the authors tell during the documentary "God knows everything but is not a snitch." In the favelas, this can mean the difference between being a drug dealer and being an activist – and that, for many, means the difference between life and death: "There wasn't Superman at the model. I never liked this idea of playing with these kinds of characters. Inside of a favela, reality is reality. If you die, you die for good" (Serra and Oliveira, 2012). The narratives continue through stories of coping and finding a way out from personal crisis and danger. Most tell how they were able to stand up thanks to a positive encounter that provided inter-subjective help and support, offering a positive model for relating to others, the perspective of creative activity, and the potential for collective action.

The life stories show correspondence between the routes of socialisation experienced by the creators and participants of *Morrinho* and those of favela dwellers. The former are not outsiders but people who belong psychologically and socially to favela communities. Whenever these creators speak about *Morrinho* they tell their own life stories. These are stories anchored in the language and reality of the favela, which they both express and overcome with their example. They are stories that mix languages of exclusion, poverty, loss, and contravention with stories of resilience, coping with failure, and, ultimately, success.

Morrinho – as an NGO – offers psychosocial scaffoldings: it acts as family, state, and private sector, developing competencies, offering support, organising job opportunities, and generating a new set of positive representations of the favelas and the city as a whole:

- It competes directly with drug traffic by offering an alternative way of life. Their actions and interpersonal supporting structures protect against marginalisation and are essential conditions for social integration;
- It is present in the voices of residents, in the manner with which they report their personal life (in particular through *TV Morrinho* but also in the exhibitions), their experience within the community (with *Morrinho Social*, where they lead workshops among other activities);
- In the relationship between the favelas and the city: with *Morrinho Tourism* they present the favela to many tourists, from Brazil and elsewhere, creating a different and better image of this specific favela; and with various small businesses, such as the hostel Pousada Favelinha and the film production company Cara de Cão Filmes, moving from the city to inside the favela;
- It performs tasks belonging to social movements, cultural enterprises (the short films produced both institutionally and commercially through *TV Morrinho*), artists (they produce the exhibitions all over the world, including the representation of Brazil at the Venice Biennale in 2007), and social workers (through *Morrinho Social*, they offer leadership community courses, including on basic notions of citizenship, the environment, and health as well as practical courses of photography and English);
- It makes use of art, culture, imagination, and creativity to subvert stereotypes, connect urban spaces, rendering the culture of favelas visible and attractive in the eyes of the city, the country, and the world (through the documentary "God knows everything but is not a snitch," public presentations on the project, and the travelling exhibition of the model of *Morrinho*, including performances);
- It builds unforeseen partnerships with social movements, media, state, and private sector (the official residency, named "O Palácio das Laranjeiras"/"The Palace of Laranjeiras" of the State Governor moved there to push favelas onto the agenda of the city and offer new lenses to read favela environments). This is visible in the number of international media publications where they are praised (TV Cultura Brasil; Globo; Rio Times Online).
- It acts as conflict mediator. They ensure access to the favelas (in particular through *Morrinho Tourism* with guided tours to the model but also in their close relationship with the hostel Pousada Favelinha) and communicate both with drug traffic and the police. They regenerate the built

environment of favelas and construct spaces for positive sociability in the city, such as the Association of the Inhabitants of Pereirão.

- The participants/co-authors have life trajectories similar to those of leaders and activists; they operate as mirror stories that reflect pathways widely found in favela communities: experiencing failure, loss, and suffering and standing up again.
- It tells various life stories as a central methodology (in *TV Morrinho* and in the documentary "God knows everything but is not a snitch") used as leverage, as a platform for identification, and as an example of survival and determination, as depositories of hope and potential futures for the other members of the community, who potentially join the Project.
- It invests in the self as a central asset for social development: social change requires individuals who understand themselves as agents and believe in their capacity to act as protagonists of their own lives.
- It uses arts and culture to connect the city and subvert negative stereotypes of the favela; they pull cultural resources, engage imagination and creativity, and showcase the culture of the favela to the city, to the country, and to the world (through *TV Morrinho* and *Morrinho Exhibition*).
- It uses resources of its local culture, in particular Brazilian black heritage, for social development and healing: sociability, joy, celebration, and potential spaces are assets always present in their films (*TV Morrinho*), exhibitions, and activities (*Morrinho Exhibition* and *Morrinho Social*) used to counteract suffering and exclusion.

As observed in the previous chapter, the idea of embedding existing cultural references in projects for social change has been studied in several programmes and respective toolkits, in particular when looking at communities that are characterised by diversity in terms of culture. A unique and significant characteristic of *Morrinho* is its organic relationship with the context of the favela: contrary to traditional models of social development where external agents propose and lead the execution of projects, or even to participatory models, where local peoples are included in decision-making processes controlled by the aid industry or the state, this project, which became an NGO, has not been built by outsiders. It emerged, developed, and is widely recognised as a product of favela territories. Activists and leadership were born, grew up, and continue to live in the favela of Pereirão and this organisation holds a strong territorial link with the specific community of Pereirão.

Nevertheless, it is not as easy and positive as it might seem and sound at first. The Project is always fighting to be sustainable and to keep the jobs they created but they fear asking too much participation of outsiders (besides sponsors and partners, which they accept very well) as they do not know the reality of the favela. They also seem to not be interested in planning in advance, which has proven to be very problematic in activities such as putting up an exhibition in another country. The project authors created Morrinho Social where they teach leadership skills so it might seem as though they would work within a structure but, most of the time, there are no roles assigned, which can also prove to be difficult when there are deadlines or tasks to be accomplished which is the case when presenting a film screening, which is one of their activities.

Even though favelas share some general characteristics, each one is unique as observed by Chico Serra (Serra and Oliveira, 2012). Children from the favela identified a (their) problem without aiming to do so or to call any attention to it. Nevertheless, against all odds, the game evolved into a work of art and from there to an NGO aiming for social change. The change aimed at is the negative perception people usually have of favelas. In Morrinho, there was never a question of needing to embed or to understand the cultural references, as here the cultural references were not seen as "other" but its own.

Morrinho might be observed as a storytelling organisation (Boyce, 1995), as it struggles to get the stories of insiders and outsiders straight, to market their activities to customers (guests), investors, and stakeholders. In the 1990s, Boje developed the idea of a storytelling organisation into a

> collective storytelling system in which the performance of stories is a key part of members' sense-making and a means to allow them to supplement individual memories with institutional memory (Boje, 1991, p. 106; Boje, 1995, p. 1000) is the collective re-historicising (memory) of the institution, the ongoing (re)negotiation as the present is unfolded into the past (attention), and the (re)visioning (expecting) the future.
>
> (Boje, 1991)

This is exactly what *Morrinho* does through its activities, which aim to deconstruct the grand narratives of the favelas.

The life trajectories of *Morrinho* creators reveal the importance of personal experience and social identification in defining the identity and method of work of *Morrinho*. Telling a life story and showcasing it as an example, exposing its determinants and experiences, its moments of decision, rupture, and choice, the lessons it can offer, and the model it can provide: this is the elementary method at the basis of all conversations and strands of the project developed by *TV Morrinho*. This method is comparable to the antenarrative method microstoria proposed by Boje (2001; to use the "little people's" histories and ignore the "great man" accounts that are most often used in organisation studies. Microstoria relies here on the life stories told by the leaders and participants of *Morrinho*, in interviews and, in particular, in *TV Morrinho*). They tell life stories, use the life stories of their creators (seen as leaders) and members as a starting point, and take them as the raw material that exemplifies how oneself and one's society combine to define a human life. These life stories are consolidated as narratives of community life and maybe even of Rio as a whole; in *TV Morrinho* their stories are told again and again as examples of survival and determination, as warnings, as containers of hope and potential futures, as alternatives to what is the case, and guidance for choices and decision-making.

Central to these life stories is that they are exemplary of favela trajectories; they operate as mirror stories that reflect and express pathways widely found in favela communities and are thus stories favela people understand and recognise well. The first and perhaps most important finding related to the identity of *Morrinho*, corroborated by all data streams of the research, is that it is an organisation solidly connected to the life-world of the favela: it was not produced outside and taken into favela environments. On the contrary, people who belong and are deeply connected to favela territories generated the territories inside the favela.

Morrinho's life stories are essentially told through *TV Morrinho*, which was created based on training the young founders of *Morrinho* in audio-visual production and the visual arts through continuous re-interpretation of reality, having video as a creative tool. *TV Morrinho*'s short videos, performed within the miniature city ("Saci at the Morrinho," "Perri's pool," "Morrinho Samba School I and II"; "Uprising of the toys"; "The end of the world at Morrinho," "Adventures in Amsterdam," among others) dissolve the boundary between documentary/fiction, functioning as auto-ethnography, confabulation every day, fictionalisation of the real, game/existence. It is no accident that interest in the project is always renewed, which is shown in the documentary feature film "God knows everything but is not a snitch" that introduces *Morrinho*, tells its story, the impact and fascination wherever it goes, and how a child's game turned into a creative process.

In "Saci at the Morrinho," 2007 (made for Nickelodeon), Master Renato's Lego figure tells the story of a baffling Saci Pererê that moved to Morrinho's favela. A sinister Saci, with cavernous voice and slang, able to scare and beat up a *Morrinho* resident for stealing candy from children. The childhood and childishness of tales and stories are being glued, fused with everyday characters of the *Morrinho*.

The video begins with a child humming at the favela when approached by an older boy, "Hey, little one, give me your sweet, lost it! Give me your sweet or I'll beat you," that ends with the Saci justice maker – one leg, pipe smoker, black boy character from the Brazilian folklore beating the older boy, adjusting the behaviour. Brazilian folklore and urban folklore are contaminated, merged, in amoral fables and stories permeated by images of the world, the cinema, and media, such as the story of the invasion of the *Morrinho* by dinosaurs, with the sound of shrill voices, howls, screams, and confusion. This mix of childish games and "naive" pranks crossed with cruelty and violence, gestures, voices that animate scenes, objects, characters: these videos raise a life that overflows the "state of life," the clichés about the slums, violence, drug dealing.

Nothing is informed, the registration of the narrator's fables (the owners of the voices of the puppets) in footage shot by the boys of *TV Morrinho* incorporated in the game (the camera is part of the game), and they put lots of tension into the scene.

In "The Revolution of the toys," 2008, by *TV Morrinho*, these tensions between real and fiction reached a sophisticated level of meta-language, when the Lego toys discover that the boys who give voice to them will travel to the Venice Biennale without taking them. They begin an uprising at the *Morrinho*/miniature city in an attempt to travel to Italy following its creators.

The set design and the scenery in *TV Morrinho* of the world of *Morrinho* are crucial in telling its stories. Houses and signs have been painted to resemble streets and the figures have been altered to portray all the real characters that interact in this favela. Even though they represent this specific favela and each one has its own social, cultural, and economic characteristics, when released internationally, they become representative of the idea of a Brazilian favela in general which is crucial in producing an effective change in general perception.

The filming in *TV Morrinho* is usually tight, so as not to give away more than the hand reaching into this world, affecting things around it. The character voiceovers are either recorded on location or redubbed later in *Morrinho*'s improvised, do-it-yourself style, studio. In this sense, *Morrinho* is Elizabethan, similar to the London Shakespeare's Globe Theatre, where a small company has to perform all the roles in their plays. The young men's disguise of their voices when taking on female characters, adds an additional theatrical dimension that is part of the presentation. Several of the films also display a level of reflexivity that is refreshing for participatory media.

In the middle of a shooting scene at the miniature city, with caveirão, Bope – the tank-like police car – shootings, confusion, threats, the toys stop the scene when they find out that the boys will travel abroad without them. They stop the scene to question the status of "toys/ workers" versus the world of artists/creators, the live work of the authors of the stories and the dead work of the toys that "stay eating flour here" while the boys travel. The toys are threatening to protest and strike, emptying the scene, creating a void of life, desertion and exodus (evade, bio-political strategy to empty power chairs): "If I'm not going to Venice, we'll stop, *Morrinho* will go bankrupt, it'll be a mess, we'll put it on the Internet and YouTube, there will be a fight if we don't go." The boys appear in the scene, enter the history of the Lego figures and decide to reconsider. The toys' original Lego figures go to Venice, not just their brand-new replicas, with no "story." The final scene: the toys are happy with their suitcases in their hands and on their backs, crossing an alley at the miniature city. Between all the tricks and jokes, they cross the path of real ants, ants and Lego figures intersect, lives outside of these signs/ remote from the lives of the objects, life images, which become pulsating, true documentaries of another category, just when crossed by fiction.

This relationship between fiction and documentary, working with clichéd images of mass culture, action movies, novels, television journalism, film, and an imaginary toy industry (as in the *TV Morrinho* film "End of the World at the Morrinho"), combining the aesthetics and values that come from the suburbs, make the production of TV Morrinho a singular one. The ability to interact with other universes also draws attention, always incorporating the elements of other cities, cultures, world views, as we see in the interaction between the boys and the *Morrinho* indigenous film-makers, Video in the Villages Project (Exchanging Glances), or in the video "Adventures in Amsterdam" where drugs appear in a totally different context to the reality of Brazilian favelas (drug dealing, violence, and death) and are shown as a safe and pleasurable experience offered in Amsterdam coffee shops, which surprises the boys.

The *TV Morrinho* films are part of the cultural production that comes from the slums and peripheries (music, theatre, dance, literature, film), emerges as a political speech which does not come from academics, researchers, the state, the media, or any political party, and puts into play new mediators and producers of culture: rappers, funk singers, b-boys, young actors, performers, residents of the slums, unemployed, underemployed, producers from the so-called informal economy, groups and discourses that are revitalising the poverty areas and reconfiguring the urban Brazilian cultural scene.

But what makes the stories of *Morrinho* so powerful? Why is this seemingly simple method, of telling stories, so successful? What makes it work? One answer might be that the problem of drug dealing was transformed into something different, something that members owned (in some cases the result could be called art – the model of *Morrinho*). The boys and girls were not interested in changing the preconceived ideas of life in a favela, but in telling stories, some of which required cooperation from the community and were than screened both in the community and nationally (and later, internationally). The films and their making were about things in and outside daily life – thus giving it an extra dimension, again without (external) ulterior motive.

Analysing the stories of *Morrinho* as a project with various branches (*TV Morrinho; Morrinho Social; Morrinho Tourism; Morrinho Exhibition*) and an NGO, it would seem to consist of some important ingredients. The (art) intervention created changed existing patterns of behaviour so boys and girls could work together. It brought new opportunities, new options (through the making of the films the teenagers started talking about their dreams for the future). The process of cooperation and getting feedback from the progress in one's own product (the films) created awareness about its quality and how that might continue to improve, making the cooperation sustainable in the aspirations for social change even if at a micro-level. In the words of Chico Serra and Cilan Oliveira:

> the artists who initiated Morrinho had a radical change in their lives: in their self-esteem, in their way of speaking and believing in themselves. Above all, it's a leisure space in the middle of community, created not by the public power or private enterprises but by its inhabitants. It's a magical space, a micro-universe inside the universe of Brazilian favelas.
>
> (Chico Serra and Cilan Oliveira, 2012)

The multidisciplinary vision within Morrinho goes beyond the exact sciences and demands dialogue with the humanities and the social sciences, as well as with art, literature, and poetry.

Social problems exemplify complexity. They comprise several sub-problems that fall into the domains of different disciplines and sectors. Moreover, there are wide variations in the preferences and values of decision-makers and stakeholders (Scheringer, Jaeger, and Esfeld, 2000). *Morrinho*'s process and history are both horizontal and vertical. It is horizontal in the cooperation of disciplines (such as cinema, social work, and visual art) at the same level during its development, the involvement of different stakeholders in a local planning process, and the cooperation of administrative bodies as Favelinha (the hostel situated in Favela Pereira da Silva) and Associação dos Moradores (Association of the residents of Favela Pereira da Silva). It is vertical in the cooperation of disciplines at different levels when development is combined with best practices in a region, *Morrinho* as an NGO and other associations cooperate, and local communities interact (Rhön and Whitelaw, 2000).

Morrinho Social existence is based on volunteering, with classes in photography and English as well as activities for children and young people from the community and outside which opens the dialogue with other communities. Even though this is positive as it shows an engagement with people external to the Project, it is also a problem as one of their aims is to create and sustain jobs. Chico Serra, one of *Morrinho*'s film makers and one of the managers of Morrinho, says that *Morrinho Social* has set the goal of offering courses in community leadership including notions of citizenship, environmental issues, and health. Leadership-development and capacity-building initiatives, like those highlighted by *Morrinho*, are key to empowering local communities so they can make the most of their assets and meet the challenges that they face. *Morrinho* continually challenges its participants and organisers to work hard at strengthening the ability of both individuals and community-based initiatives to make a profound difference in their neighbourhood:

> Morrinho is always a work in progress, it's always evolving as its community. The daily life of Morrinho is a mixture of this maintenance job and the activities in and out of the community. At the moment, we have just finished a workshop that lasted three months, a teaching experience for community correspondents, in a partnership between Viva Favela and Viva Rio. We taught young people from the community to produce and edit videos, produced three documentaries and a making of [for a film]. The exhibitions take place more by invitation than by self-initiative.
>
> (Chico Serra and Cilan Oliveira, 2012).

The main goal of *Morrinho Social* is to offer a change to the community of Pereira da Silva, being a source of communication of the positive side of life in a favela as well as opening up a place for cultural encounters in the community through activities such as film screenings, talks, and workshops. The courses and workshops have been proved necessary and important as this helps in the perception of what a favela might be for its inhabitants as well as the surrounding communities. Through the lenses of art history, the project is comparable to the recent interest of contemporary artists in daily life and society in what has been termed social practice and relational aesthetics (Bourriaud, 1998). As many contemporary artists' projects, *Morrinho* presents a sort of micro-utopia or a desired world. Although this world is based on real-life stories, it is not a projection of what it could be. In this sense, it can be seen from the perspective of art as a social system, where an art project can make observations of the reality and show a perception of it that then, is subject to other observations and perceptions.

The third strand of the project, *Morrinho Tourism*, is where these second observations are made more directly. Unlike the favela tours that parade tourists on the backs of trucks through the streets of Rocinha, mentioned before as the largest favela in Rio de Janeiro and Latin America, *Morrinho* guides visitors to Pereira da Silva on foot to see first-hand their creation. The visits to the site are crucial for a better understanding of what a favela might mean and to contribute to a true perception of the artistic creativity coming out of the communities. A visit to the model of *Morrinho*, in its 350 square meters, with its creators, and a guided tour to the favela contribute to an understanding of the creativity and reach of *Morrinho*.

The model has been recreated in many countries, which is very important for the international perception of *Morrinho* and its community as well as favelas in general. Although, a visit to the site of the actual model is striking in the way that it translates the reality of a favela with the stories it embodies. Project members have also produced a line of merchandising comprising T-shirts, hats, photographs, postcards, and DVDs. All funds go to the social initiatives of *Morrinho* and the community. The tours to the model include a narration of the history and stories of the Project by one of its members, an explanation of the different compositions of the model, and the screening of some of the videos produced by *TV Morrinho*. These visits are, of course, very important for the project's aims and as a means of financing it. But it is also important to note that these visits are sometimes the result of curiosity with experiencing something different or exotic and the perception of the public is not always the same as the one intended by the guides, which leads us back to Luhmann's idea of art as a social system.

Morrinho Exhibition is where the founders and the successive generations of youth take *Morrinho* into the streets, internationally, to construct small versions of their hillside. It can be described as a living exhibition with passing people watching in wonder while a bank of sand and a pile of bricks is eventually grown into a small village. When abroad, the *Morrinho* group sometimes invites other youth to join them in the construction process, teaching others a valuable lesson in participatory arts practice as well as changing the perspective of the traditional idea of a favela and its community.

Morrinho Exhibition consists of the construction of the model of 350 square meters of the Favela Pereira da Silva and the screening of the videos produced by TV *Morrinho*. The first exhibition was made for Mira – Mostra Internacional de Arquitetura (International Exhibition of Architecture), in Rio de Janeiro together with the works of Oscar Niemeyer, Lúcio Costa, and Jean Nouvel. Later, *Morrinho* built models in Fórum Mundial das Culturas (Universal Forum for Cultures), in Barcelona (2004), Point Ephémère, in Paris (2005), and, by invitation of Robert Storr, *Morrinho* built a 200 square meter model representing Brazil in the 52nd Venice Biennale (2007), achieving the status of social and art work.

Morrinho is, besides a project, a community-based organisation, with collaboration at its core: each individual shares a different knowledge of the different initiatives (from TV production to exhibitions and guided tours to tourism). Through a multidisciplinary and collaborative approach, they manage to get continuous involvement of the community, making the project more appealing and sustainable, even if facing difficulties, because when one part of the project does not work as it should, there is always another part of the project that supports it. This diversity of interests represents a moving away from the academia, the introversion of modernism, and the belief of "art for the sake of art." It is remaking networks and realigning narratives to make contact with the pulse of wider social, disciplinary, and cultural change and not simply formal innovation.

Nevertheless, they seem to fear the idea of planning and involving outsiders, from whatever disciplinary field they might be, in such plans, in the long-term activities of the project. They collaborate with outsiders in partnerships and volunteers, but always on a short-term basis and never as members. The only exception was with the long relationship and collaboration with the film makers who made "God knows everything but is not a snitch," probably because it was a trust relationship coming from the film makers towards the children. Interestingly, they, who are fighting a preconceived idea – or grand narrative – (in this case, of the favela), themselves show preconceived ideas towards outsiders to the favela's world. Not everybody shows prejudice towards the favela and its inhabitants but it is a grand narrative that outsiders, in general, fear and avoid the favela – a grand narrative with which they seem to agree. The same goes for the involvement of various disciplines: they came to regard themselves as artists and they seem to have embedded the same grand narratives attached to arts to scientific disciplines, putting completely aside ideas of planning and chaos management as well as displaying a total ignorance about the interest science has in creativity and chaos, despite the different ways of looking at it.

Currently, *Morrinho* has more in common with members of tenants and action groups, radical planners, and cultural geographers, than it does with artists as in its early stages. Similarly, in comparable projects, artists dealing with issues of gender or sexuality may have links with communities dealing with those issues. Likewise, certain black artists may have more interest in the issue of racism and other matters affecting them and their communities directly, than they have in other discourses of other artists with different concerns. This story is a welcome change in the culture landscape of Brazil and marks *Morrinho* as an essential transformative multidisciplinary and collaborative project.

Analysis of the characteristics, methods, and actions of *Morrinho* shows that they are sui generis and innovative. Their explicit aims are recognition of the culture and rich potential of favela life-worlds, the demolition of urban barriers, and the dialogical crossings that can produce transformative changes both in the public sphere and in social and individual subjectivities. They openly compete with the drug trade for influence in the routes of socialisation open to young favela people and work as mediators of conflict in disputes between the drug factions, the police, and favela dwellers. Their range of actions is extensive, engaging both favela communities and the larger public sphere of the city. They put emphasis on the regeneration of the built environment of favelas, on the construction of spaces for positive sociability and conviviality, and on psychosocial interventions that aim to foster self-esteem, self-control, and awareness for the transformation of individual and collective trajectories.

The structuring of everyday life takes a central role in the communities' perception and is seen as vital for avoiding criminality and engaging people in meaningful activity. Participants explicitly say that *Morrinho* gives them something to do, something to commit to, an opportunity to be responsible, to establish markers in the week and in the day so as to frame everyday life. Routine, structure, activity are all described systematically by participants through the folk understanding that it is necessary to occupy one's time. In the talk of participants there is robust presence of metaphors related to the family, as when they state that *Morrinho* is like "a family." Their most important action, referred to again and again, is to "give a hand," to talk and to help, taking people away from the route of crime: Cilan says that "there were times when there were 30 boys here wanting to play. They wanted a space at the model. They wanted to make their own shack" (Serra and Oliveira, 2012). In this way, Morrinho grew to be much larger than anything Cilan claims he could have done alone "As a team, we've constructed more than 40 favelas of pure creativity; I could not have done this all by myself" (Serra and Oliveira, 2012).

Under the motto "initiating a small revolution," *Morrinho* has created, through collaboration and the integration of different knowledge of each individual within the community as well as from external partners in activities, a space for the community. It offers social change to the community of Pereira da Silva, trying to be a communication source of the positive side of life in the favelas, as well as a space for encounters in social and cultural terms by promoting activities such as film screenings and debates, local and internationally. This promotion is rather passive as they attract attention from outsiders through their aesthetics and stories, but they do not look actively for partnerships and they seem to lack understanding of how to present themselves to potential stakeholders, especially when comes to specific aims and goals and the benefits of involvement for stakeholders.

Against the negative scenery of favelas, *Morrinho*'s achievement in creating powerful images to counter the solid course of frequent negative coverage of Rio de Janeiro's favelas is of great importance here. Despite the relevance of informal building settlements, Rio de Janeiro's huge favelas somewhat still disturb the city's image, not so much because of how they look, but because of what they represent to Brazilians but also to foreigners. Favelas are the consequence of Rio de Janeiro's (and any city) inability to accommodate all its citizens, both physically and culturally. The bad impression is not completely inaccurate in certain places, but it demands a price on favela residents, most of whom are not involved in the drug-related violence that fills the news. With *Morrinho* attracting intense media interest in Brazil and abroad throughout the years for its aesthetics and the ingenuity of its child creators, growing from a local phenomenon to a popular international exhibit, this positive coverage means a chance to bridge the gap between the neighbourhood's perception and its reality, and to bestow the neighbourhood with a strong feeling of pride and belonging: "Projeto Morrinho is the reason that tourists who come to Rio visit Pereirão, which generates income for the community," says Kelly Martins, a 34-year-old who worked at the *Morrinho* project before taking a job as head of the Pereira da Silva residents' association.

Morrinho challenges many of our society's deepest assumptions, built upon the power of artistic creation and expression to spark new ideas, catalyse critical thinking, elicit new actions, inspire individuals, and create visions. Whether intentionally conceived or not, multidisciplinarity (in this case, a combination of arts, new media, journalism, and others, as stated before) here becomes a political act with *Morrinho* as the global ambassadors.

It is a small revolution, if a revolution can be small. *Morrinho* started as a children's game, it became an art work which made it jump to an NGO and, today, it gives jobs to more than 20 young people living in the community of Pereira da Silva, in Rio de Janeiro. It cannot be compared to a small enterprise despite the numbers. More than giving jobs, this project is about showing a different meaning of favela. With hard work, they managed to reproduce the model in Brazil, the USA, and Europe. Wherever it goes, despite its management difficulties, it makes people wonder about the hidden stories of a favela, which are much more than the preconceived ideas we are all used to.

Notes

1 Open Museum programme: programmes designed for groups with special educational needs.
2 CAM – Modern Art Centre, Gulbenkian Foundation was founded in 1983 and existed under this name until 2016, when it became Gulbenkian Museum. In the analysis of this Project, created under CAM, the choice was to keep the former name of the institution.

3 Diagnóstico Social do Município da Amadora, Rede Social, Gabinete de Acção Social da Câmara Municipal da Amadora, 2008
4 Diagnóstico Social do Município da Amadora, Rede Social, Gabinete de Acção Social da Câmara Municipal da Amadora, 2008
5 HUD is the US Department of Housing and Urban Development, which supports projects in a variety of fields working in the realm of housing and urban development: "HUD's mission is to create strong, sustainable, inclusive communities and quality affordable homes for all. HUD is working to strengthen the housing market to bolster the economy and protect consumers; meet the need for quality affordable rental homes: utilize housing as a platform for improving quality of life; build inclusive and sustainable communities free from discrimination; and transform the way HUD does business." (In http://portal.hud.gov/ last checked March 25, 2013.)
6 *Favela* trees are a typical plant of the Catinga region, in Bahia, resistant to the long, dry period to which they are submitted.
7 "Inter-American Development Bank funded this US$180 million 'slum to neighborhood' project in 1995 in which it sought to integrate existing *favela*s into the fabric of the city through infrastructure upgrading and service increases. The project involves 253,000 residents in 73 communities. Key to the success of this large project was a committed and flexible city government and the use of intra- and extra-institutional partnerships with NGOs, the private sector, churches, and the general population. Especially instrumental was the use of grass-roots level infrastructure upgrading experts as project managers who could work easily with both the government and with the community members." Retrieved from http://web.mit.edu/urbanupgrading/upgrading/case-examples/ce-BL-fav.html 21 August 2012.
8 "Rio Cidade Project was part of an urban intervention established in Rio, between 1995 and 2000, following the 90s urban investments, with strong influence from the politics applied at American and European cities, like Barcelona. 'Rio Cidade' was part of one of the projects included in Rio de Janeiro's City Strategy, under the subtitle 'the urbanism is back to the city'. This plan was worked out on Cesar Maia's council administration (1993–1996) and it was concluded in September, 1995." Retrieved from http://www.ub.edu/geocrit/-xcol/338.htm 21 August 2012.
9 *Favelados* is the term for the people who live in *favela*s. However, it is commonly applied in a pejorative way to poor people in general, in the Brazilian context.
10 AfroReggae and Cufa are hybrid organisations that offer psychosocial scaffoldings: they act as family, state, and private sector, developing competencies, offering support, organising job opportunities, and generating a new set of positive representations of the favelas and the city as a whole (Unesco, 2012).

4 Integrating three important disciplines in art and cultural projects for social change

Art: the empowering effect of creativity

From the relationship between the theoretical framework presented in Chapters 1 and 2 and the practical examples (*Intervene: Heroes and Villains; Project Row Houses; Morrinho*) that enlighten the role of art in projects for social change, the empowering potential of creativity becomes clear.

The first observation made in Chapter 2 was that art making is considered to be a universal human behaviour, which has always been a part of our personal and interpersonal communication (Malchiodi, 2007). More interestingly, as this relates to the projects analysed and their contemporary context, it was observed that in recent decades artists have gradually enlarged the boundaries of art, taking the relationship between art and the social to a new level, as they have wanted to engage with an increasingly pluralistic environment alternating between the everyday and the unusual, the analytical and the critical. This pluralism of interests in art representations and interpretations is revealing of the focus of art on critically observing and intervening in society and its culture.

Looking at the history of art, Breton's concept of the independence of art related to the role of art and culture in class society (Breton and Rivera, 1938) and might be understood as a view of art as social system. It reflected the idea that art can only have a social role if it is free from the logic of domination. Only in this way, according to their manifesto, could it contribute to a free society that shows an activist response towards exploitation and domination and where individuals can freely associate and determine themselves. In this way, the manifesto is a clear criticism of fascism and Stalinism, two dictatorships suffocating artistic expression as they were drowning workers' opposition, but it was also a comment on the role of art and culture in the social realm. The manifesto opposed the abstract idea that art could somehow be neutral in a class-based society.

If art as a social system is looked at through the lenses of social sciences, then, the role of art appears to be more passive. Some researchers and academics argue that certain social systems have the power to regulate both the form and content of art. According to Luhmann, there would be no other system in society that does what art does but, according to his point of view, art is reduced and concerned with a specific part or state of society. In such approaches, art might be considered as a mere echo of the state of the economy, or of the state of the political system. Lukács shows another view: he argues that reality exists objectively and independently of consciousness, and, therefore, cognition would be a reflection of reality. In the same way, art would have to be a factual reflection of the totality of reality, and not a critical reflection, providing an image of reality where the opposition between essence and appearance of reality is given in a natural union. Although, each artwork would have to be a closed universe that advances a more complete and livelier reflection of reality than the recipients have, it would have to capture the fluctuations and inexhaustibility of reality. For doing so, the role of art would not be to portray individual persons and situations, but representative characters under representative social and cultural contexts. Art would have to convey a rich expression of the experiences of life; for doing so it would require a propaganda character and would have to educate the masses, under a political agenda, as in Stalinism (Lukács, 1954).

In traditional theories, art is seen as a system representing unlimited values that surpass society, being considered as a system with a high position in relation to other social systems (Fuchs, 2018). Art as a social system, in sociology, implies that society is a social system with various subsystems and each one is autonomous with one unique function in society. Therefore, one social system would never do the same as another social system. Following this line of thought, art is considered a functioning, closed system and would work autonomously from other social systems, implying that no other system in society does what art does. The function of art, as a system, in modern society would be to, through perception and communication, show a reality that can be observed. The evolution of art is fully determined by its own logic; there would be no external influences from other social systems or society (Luhmann, 1995).

Bourdieu also speaks of the autonomy of art and believes that if we confine ourselves only to the consideration of the codes of the field of art, we fail to see that the dominating codes in this field correspond to the cultural interests, lifestyle, and habitus of the higher social classes (1984). In other words, questions concerning cultural domination and cultural power relations remain outside the phenomenological analysis. This is something that many contemporary artists making art projects for social change seem to dismiss: the cultural power relations.

In this sense, when attempting to understand the ideas of participation and empowerment in a specific community with its own cultural references, Arsenault's study with LLILAS and Texas Performing Arts under the Fulbright-Hays Group Projects Abroad Programme brings light to the research. The study looked at young people's performance art-making focused on the role of the performing arts in educational and social projects in Brazil. This American study concluded that these projects demonstrate that the arts can foster a sense of empowerment through dignity and self-esteem and play an important role in providing opportunities for education and employment. The conclusions of the study show that economic forms of empowerment where people gain jobs and economic benefit link directly to individual feelings of self-confidence and personal empowerment and that art projects can have a positive role by boosting self-confidence, with the feeling that "everybody is (can be) an artist," claimed by Joseph Beuys in the 1970s. This suggests that when playing the role of artists, people tend to produce objects in many forms, which can range from films to actual objects, music, and performance. As observed in *Project Row Houses* and in *Morrinho*, real jobs can come out of participatory and creative practices, which reflects both at economic and psychological levels.

Looking back at the theoretical framework presented in Chapters 1 and 2, it is possible to identify two main different ways of interpreting the relation of art and society, in particular when thinking of social change: the art history approach and the sociological approach. Each discipline or approach is not consensual and there are different trends in each, which look at art as more of an active agent of change and others regarding art as a more passive agent. Despite having a more active or passive role in society, all these approaches look at the idea of the perspective/perception that art gives about the world and how this can have an effect on society. One conclusion emerging from these theories of art as a social system is that art can have both an active and passive role in society but, either way, it will always allow for different perspectives which will lead more to uncertainty than to providing definitive answers on what can be done in terms of society.

The second strand analysed in the theoretical framework – art as social practice, Chapter 1 – shows that the literature referring to the term social practice links it with ideas of participation, the possible role of art in society with a focus on the relation and combination of art with other disciplines – ideas that came up when analysing *Morrinho*.

From all the attempts to create a line of thought and put in words the possible meanings of art as a social practice, the book *Relational Aesthetics* (1998), by Nicolas Bourriaud, which puts the tone on participation, has come to be seen as a major text for a generation of artists and art critics who came to notoriety in Europe in the early to mid 1990s (Bishop, 2006) but also for researchers and students.

Relational art, to Bourriaud (1998), is seen as a response to the virtual relationships of the Internet and globalisation, which on the one hand have prompted a desire for more physical and face-to-face interaction between people, while on the other have inspired artists to adopt a do-it-yourself (DIY) approach to model their own worlds. This culture of do-it-yourself is very present in self-initiated projects such as *Project Row Houses* and *Morrinho* and, in this sense, this culture might be regarded as a trope to build transformative possibilities which challenge perceptions and grand narratives. Through an empowerment of the artists and people involved in the "doing" of the projects, these endeavours become better possibilities per se or, in Bourriaud's words, "possible universes" (1998).

To Bourriaud, the main difference between contemporary art before and after relational aesthetics is the shift in attitude towards social change: instead of a "utopian" agenda, relational artists seek a micro-utopia as they only long to find provisional solutions in the here and now. Even though these solutions take place in a social context and within a limited timeframe, many artistic projects refuse the idea of an ending (projects, as defined by project management, have a set start and end), which in many cases also implies a lack of planning as well as sustainability.

Maybe if specific goals, within a timeframe, were set from the beginning, projects could be closer to achieving actual change in the present and be relevant locally. As Bourriaud put it, "it seems more pressing to invent possible relations with our neighbours in the present than to bet on happier tomorrows" (Bourriaud, 1998, p. 45). The problem with Bourriaud's assumption is that it seems to overlook the outcomes of these micro-utopias in the future of the communities where they take place. In other words, these projects seem to dismiss the evaluation phase, which implies the understanding of the real impact these projects may have.

Curator Maria Lind speaks about art in relation to the social and political spheres demonstrated by works and multidisciplinary projects by artists in critical points of view that range from passing a message to asking for participation which, in some cases, means taking real political action (Lind, 2011). This reveals that the interest of art in acting in society is not as naive as it might seem at first sight, as artists are shifting their roles of artists to urban planners and community workers and, more importantly, looking for collaborations as they understand that, alone, they might not be able to produce effective social change.

As the social remains a recurring theme in artistic practice, art history, and as study programmes of art schools, art historians and art critics claim the urgency to understand and locate the border of art's integration and relation with the social. This relation of art and social practice is a recurring theme and the understanding of its history and the focus on participation, empowerment, and collaboration should be taken into consideration when both critically analysing and implementing projects for social change.

In the research path, it was observed that the concept of social sculpture was often associated with the projects analysed and has also been identified as a historical inspiration for today's relation of art and social practice in both theory and practice. Robert Storr compared *Morrinho* to a social sculpture (2007) while *Project Row Houses* has been associated with the same concept by its author, Rick Lowe (2012). The term social sculpture, coined by the German artist Joseph Beuys (1921–1986), was directed at a kind of artwork that would take place in the social realm, and that, in order to be complete, would need social engagement and the participation of an audience (Kuoni, 1990). This implies a type of art that can only exist in the social realm and with the participation of an audience. It goes further in implying that such type of art can create effective social change by turning spectators (or passive citizens) into participants (or active citizens), who would become the catalysis of social sculpture. In this process of release of popular creativity, society would be transformed.

Beuys is the initiator of the trend that "everybody is an artist" by claiming that everything should be approached creatively and this would only be possible when all humans – despite their academic, professional, social, political, and economic backgrounds – consider themselves as creative agents of society and act as such. This can be seen in contemporary projects for social change – many are self-initiated and become regarded as artistic even when art is not present as a discipline but more as a creative tool to make the project work. It is also interesting to see that disciplines, such as engineering and project management, that are usually regarded as more pragmatic and averse to chaos, defending the importance of planning, also take into great consideration the importance of creativity, which is usually understood as inherent to arts only. By claiming that we are all artists, Beuys defended the participation of all people, in a collaborative practice and, subsequently, a multidisciplinary practice.

From a theoretical point of view, the relationship between art and the social realm seems to be very positive and important and it seems that there is little research regarding the reasons behind the problems encountered in art projects for social change. When analysing art projects for social change, it becomes clear that, in practice, there are several problems when trying to create effective social change through an art project, even when it shows a multidisciplinary approach with collaboration between people from different academic and professional backgrounds. This is probably due to the misunderstandings and preconceived ideas between disciplines in the current and existing multidisciplinary discourse in contrast to a broader discourse.

Project *Intervene: Heroes and Villains*, previously discussed, presented itself as multidisciplinary where the relations between the disciplines were thought of logically as interdependence and complementarity. Nevertheless, the disciplines involved are mainly artistic – at a formal level, the project evolved in the areas of theatre, photography, and video. These areas were used as a form of promoting a critical and creative reflection around the idea of construction of the self. It was also important to work with psychologists and social workers but most of the project was based in practical work, developing from direct contact with the art works of the collection and the temporary exhibitions at CAM – Gulbenkian Foundation. Such focus on the formal results proved to be a problem at different levels, including in bringing children from their area of residence to the museum. Rather than creating activities in the community, involving other residents from outside the focus group but related to them, the project was mainly based in the museum, assuming that taking the children to the museum would be part of the solution. It seems that there was a lack of understanding of the cultural references of the community subject to the project. More importantly, it seems that the project could have benefited with both a thorough understanding of the cultural references of the community as well as embedding and integrating the existing cultural references in the project.

The Theatre of the Oppressed theory and methodology as well as the video and photography work developed under the theme of Heroes and Villains, in *Intervene*, were of the utmost importance in changing the self-perception of the young participants as they were empowered through participation and decision-making during the project. This was an engine for achieving self-confidence that became evident in a major effort to become someone who could not only change individually (which in this case would be converted into not dropping out of school at an early age) but also contribute to producing effective change in his or her community. Here it was possible to see, in practical terms, through a project, how empowerment through creative tools can prove to be an efficient way to create a change in self-perception.

This question of self-perception and empowerment was also raised in *Project Row Houses*. Rick Lowe started the project in 1993 having in mind the artistic, cultural, and economic development of the Third Ward. After studying the architecture of the houses and their history in social and cultural terms, which reflected diverse, self-contained African-American communities, Lowe decided to refurbish them as a new form of art, cultural, and social action among the community. The assumption of Lowe was that the site could provide both a powerful and accessible material link to the African-American past and a setting within which the work of contemporary African-American artists could be produced and accessible to the African-American community of the Third Ward.

Ultimately, the houses were transformed into affordable homes for single mothers and artists-in-residence, while maintaining their architectural integrity. In this way, Lowe has rewritten the traditional narrative of urban redevelopment by locating the shotgun houses as a focal and empowering point of the Third Ward, an element to be celebrated and linked to cultural traditions in the face of processes that seek to remove poor and working-class residents. The aim of the project was to change the perception people usually have from this area which is, in part, related to the poor knowledge of the rich, cultural background and true meaning of the shotgun houses, commonly associated with crime. By changing the aesthetics of the place, Rick Lowe assumed that it would get a different perception from outsiders and would draw the attention of local authorities to the importance of its artistic and cultural background and show them that the residents are part of its history and should not be removed. This was true, partially. But there was another problem, which was the need to change, in a more profound way, the living conditions of the residents of the Third Ward.

Influenced by Beuys's social sculpture, *Project Row Houses* is founded on the principle that art creates a community, in a social activity, and that this can be the foundation for revitalising depressed, inner-city neighbourhoods.

The programmes and activities at *Project Row Houses* advocate that art and creativity should be viewed as an integral part of life, exemplified in African cultural traditions wherein art is interwoven into the very fabric of life through rituals and ceremonial activities. Through artists, the project provides opportunities to identify issues. Then, through the organisation of *Project Row Houses*, creative solutions are sought. The community and its residents become the content for artists and the organisation. For many of the artists working in the Third Ward community, this is one of their primary focuses; on the one hand, the culture of the community becomes integral to the work and, on the other, the artists become integral to the community in addressing problems (Lowe, 2012). The community is empowered through art and the creation of spaces for creativity, which here clearly goes beyond the artistic realm. While creativity is key, creating strategies to generate jobs and afford-able house rents, art is only part of the solution together with other disciplines including management and urban planning.

In fact, *Project Row Houses* exists comfortably between the worlds of art, culture, and project management:

> The multi-layering of the different ways of seeing, i.e., artists, architects, community members, historians, arts administrators, developers, etc., gave the project a complexity that was more natural than if it was devel-oped strictly by artists or architects. If it was not for the multiple interests in the project, I'm not sure if it would have been sustainable or on-going. It's expected for artists or architects to think about the "final" product of their work, but when community interest, i.e., residents, city government, historian, administrators, etc., are truly connected to the project, the vitality of the project becomes creatively responding to the issues and challenges brought forth by the community. Not in the refinement of the final product.

> (Lowe, 2012)

Going back to the idea of empowerment and its relationship with the arts, the observation of projects such as *Morrinho* shows that economic forms of empowerment make people more self-confident. *Morrinho* started as a chil-dren's game, with no intention of becoming a project or an organisation. Although, from a game it evolved into an artwork (representing Brazil at the Venice Bienniale in 2007 and touring as an exhibition in Europe, the USA, and Brazil) and became an NGO aiming for social change in terms of the perception of what a favela might mean. When the then children were given cameras to visually document their stories, they felt empowered through the trust the film makers deposited in them. They produced short films and kept on working more and more on the aesthetics of *Morrinho*, the 350-square meter model of the favela. In many of the short films, they tell their roles of artists and how important it was to be in Venice with other artists. This shows how relevant the art aspect of the project was for the development of the project as an organisation – the NGO was initially created to protect the authorial rights of its initiators as artists – and hence, the importance of the perception it created in outsiders in terms of what these people could do. This perception was not only external but also internal as with the creation of the NGO, jobs were also created and today many people living in the favela of Pereirão make their living from the work they develop at *Morrinho*. With their jobs as film makers, producers, artists, tour guides, and teachers, they see the power they can have in changing the perception of a wide public regarding the grand narratives associated with favelas.

In this research, in the observation of a series of artistic projects and analysing the theoretical framework, one possible conclusion that arose is that art gives a series of perspectives on reality but those can be both right or wrong, they are mere perspectives and they do not necessarily serve a pedagogical or a transformational (for the better) agenda. In many cases, the way that art perceives the world and the way it communicates it can be helpful when aiming for social change, as in showing perspectives it also shows alternatives and possibilities of looking at the same thing as it is but from different perspectives. In the case of *Morrinho*, one of the main ideas is that a favela can be culturally seen as a place of criminality and poverty, but this perception can be changed and a favela can, at the same time, also be regarded as a place for creativity and social transformation. The multi-layered narratives of *Morrinho* share the conclusions of *Intervene: Heroes and Villains, Row Houses* and Beuys's social sculpture: we are all artists in the sense that we all have the creative potential to act in society. If we do use this power collectively is our individual responsibility.

Cultural studies: existing cultural references matter

The history of cultural studies shows its political commitment, perspectives, and strategies (Kellner, 1997). The two dominant schools of this discipline (Frankfurt School and Birmingham School) – despite their different approaches – agree that culture is not only a form of resistance to capitalist society but also a mode of social reproduction. Both schools subvert existing academic boundaries by combining social theory, politics, cultural analysis, and critique in projects aimed at a comprehensive criticism of the present configuration of culture and society. Moreover, both schools attempt to link theory and practice in a project that is oriented towards fundamental social change. Here, it is possible to find a link with the history of art.

In contemporary art, as observed in the conceptual framework outlined in Chapter 1, social practice became a key idea in the writings and practices of art. In the *Living as Form* 2011 exhibition catalogue, curator Maria Lind locates art as a social practice outside the frame of art movements: "unlike its avant-garde predecessors such as Russian Constructivism, Futurism, Situationism, Tropicalia, Happenings, Fluxus, and Dadaism, socially engaged art is not an art movement." Furthermore, she argues "these cultural practices indicate a new social order – ways of life that emphasise participation, challenge power, and span disciplines ranging from urban planning and community work to theatre and the visual arts" (Lind, 2011).

These recent turns in cultural studies and art are subverting existing academic boundaries by combining theory and practice as well as different disciplines in a project aimed at a critical analysis of culture and society. Hence, collaborative, multidisciplinary, and participatory discourses need to be understood – in theory as well as in practical cases – in their potential for social change.

One important thing that the theory and practical cases in these discourses illustrate is how crucial the embedding of existing cultural references is for success in the endeavour of transforming society. In "The Cultural Diversity Lens: A practical tool to integrate culture in development – Pedagogical Guide" the relationship between respecting the existing cultural references and success in acting upon it is underlined. "Dialogue with the populations concerned, taking their culture into account and respecting their human rights – particularly their cultural rights – are essential to the success of all projects, programmes or policies." Furthermore, the UNESCO guide asserts, "the exchanges help to diversify approaches and development models" (UNESCO, 2011).

This idea of integrating the other's culture in a project aiming at social change is, as observed in the projects described in the previous chapter, a contested field. Whereas Karl Deutsch defines integration as the creation of peace zones and "the attainment, within a territory, of a 'sense of community' and of institutions and practices strong enough and widespread enough to assure, for a 'long' time, dependable expectations of 'peaceful change' among its population" (Deutsch et al., 1957), Ernst B. Haas, defines integration as a process "whereby political actors in several distinct national settings are persuaded to shift their loyalties, expectations and political activities toward a new centre, whose institutions possess or demand jurisdiction over the pre-existing national states" (Haas, 1958). Both versions of integration imply a type of merging between two conflicting entities from which emerges one new form.

When observing the projects described in the previous chapter, one of the problems identified was the failure in understanding and embedding the existent cultural references in the process of social change – it is not that the projects did not (intentionally) disrespect the culture of the communities where they were applied but more that they ignored how crucial it is to integrate them when aiming at social change.

In the case of project *Intervene: Heroes and Villains*, the main aim of the project was to prevent early-age dropout from school. In order to do so, it was necessary to understand the reasons behind this early-age dropout in the specific community as it is not a general problem in Lisbon but it is a serious problem in the suburbs of Lisbon as well as in the suburban areas of various other big cities in Portugal.

The project showed short-term aims with high expectations of future developments but lacked a deep study of the cultural references of this community for its concretisation. The very fact that children drop out from school in large numbers and at early ages leads back to the fundamental questions of the meaning of education in different contexts and what role it plays in different social, economic, and cultural settings. Some of the questions implied by the project included: Why should families make efforts to keep their children in school at all? What is the importance of education in their lives? And how does going to school, the educational project, fit together with other, perhaps more urgent, things to do in life? This leads to a number of other basic questions. In order to understand the significance of education for different social groups (in this case, with the specificity of the Zambujal neighbourhood with its history and geography) we must know something about the capacity of these groups to make use of the education system. What, then, are the economic, social, and cultural resources that different families or social groups have at their disposal when they try to make use of school? Economic resources include such things as having money to pay for schooling (school fees, text books, clothes, in urban areas nowadays also bribes, etc.) and being able to do without the labour force of children during the time used for school. Social resources are such things as having useful contacts (for example, close relatives in town when children have nowhere to go when parents are working and school classes finish), or not being subject to social prejudice when belonging a cultural minority. Cultural resources also means the kind of cultural competence a family can have that normally only comes with higher education, such as being able to read and write or knowing what goes on in school and in the education system. This cultural competence both enables the children to survive in the classroom, and makes it possible for their parents to deal with school problems when they occur. Admittedly, these are very general questions and attempting to answer them would imply an enormous research study, which was not the case in this project. It is not that the project implementation needed more than the planned nine months. But it seems that it might have benefited from more research time, in terms of cultural references, prior to the implementation of the project. This leads to the question of the importance of project management, which will be looked at further in the following section.

In the case of *Project Row Houses*, there was a long pre-study before the implementation of the project to integrate the existing cultural references. In fact, that was one of the mottos of the project. After studying the architecture of the houses and their history in social and cultural terms, which reflected diverse, self-contained African-American communities, Lowe decided to refurbish them as a new form of art, cultural, and social action among the community. The assumption of Lowe was that the site could provide both a powerful and accessible material link to the African-American past and a setting within which the work of contemporary African-American artists could be produced and accessible to the African-American community of the Third Ward. Ultimately, the houses were transformed into affordable homes for single mothers and artists-in-residence, while maintaining their architectural integrity. In this way, Lowe has rewritten the traditional narrative of urban redevelopment by locating the shotgun houses as a focal point of the Third Ward, an element to be celebrated and linked to cultural traditions in the face of processes that seek to remove poor and working-class residents. This was a great achievement and, with that, the project managed to change the perception that outsiders had towards this community. Although, when questioned about the results of the project, the community members promptly said they still needed jobs (Lowe, 2012).

It seems, however, that the project focused more on the past, in terms of cultural references, than on the present and it failed to understand the practical needs of the community. This was corrected later and the team evaluates results on a regular basis to improve the project over time. Since their inception, *Project Row Houses* has grown both in terms of spatial and activities: from the original one and a half to six blocks, and from 22 to 40 houses. These include 12 artist exhibition and artist-in-residency spaces, seven houses for young mothers (the Young Mothers Residential Program at Project Row Houses provides housing and counselling on personal growth and parenting skills), office spaces, a community gallery, a park, and low-income residential and commercial spaces, which gave actual jobs to the people in the community. Project Row Houses can be described today as a public art project, which encourages art production but also as "art and cultural education, historic preservation, neighbourhood revitalization and community service" (Tucker, 1995). Even though there was an interest and preoccupation towards the existing cultural references, the analysis failed to understand the problems of the present and what were both the actual present and envisioned future needs.

Morrinho was initiated from within the community, implying in its inception and as its core the integration of existing cultural references and a full understanding of what change was, in fact, needed. Creators and participating members were born and/or brought up in the favelas of Rio, exposed to broken homes and to poverty, used to confrontation with the police and to the violence and loss caused by the drug trade. Most did not finish school, and those who did mention issues of access and quality of education. In the films of *TV Morrinho* and in interviews, they tell personal histories where failure, loss, poverty, racism, and discrimination were frequently experienced. Contained in the background narrative are situations of desperation that produce intense personal crises. These include the loss of loved ones, being close to death and to entering the drug trade, and attempted suicide. The situations described above were part of the problems identified in this favela by the creators of the project – the drug dealing, the crime, the loss of loved ones, and the personal crisis in terms of self-perception. This is something that might be analysed from the outside but can only be truly felt on the inside.

The children who initiated *Morrinho* were left alone most of the day, as their parents would go to their jobs, and they would play and, eventually, they started building a model of a favela, probably as a subconscious means to understand it from the outside, or from a distance. As described in the previous chapter, it became a work of art and, after, an NGO. The NGO, in many ways, works as parents by proxy. Mentoring people, offering them strong role models and emotional support alongside educational and training opportunities, is what ultimately allows re-writing of life stories as some of the authors tell during the documentary "God knows everything but is not a snitch." In the favelas, this can mean the difference between being a drug dealer and being an activist – and that, for many, means the difference between life and death. In some ways, this can be compared to the idea of the *Project Intervene – Heroes and Villains*, where there was a shift in the perception of what might be good and bad. In favelas, the respected ones are the villains. Although, *Morrinho* showed the power of being a hero, of having a job and a project where the aim was not only giving jobs to the favelados but, most importantly, to change the self-perception of the favelados and, consequently, from the outsiders and the preconceived ideas of what a favela's life might encompass in reality. They have life trajectories similar to the ones of leaders and activists; they operate as mirror stories that reflect pathways widely found in favela communities: experiencing failure, loss, and suffering and standing up again.

A unique and significant characteristic of *Morrinho* is its organic relation with the context of the favela: contrary to traditional models of social development where external agents propose and lead the execution of projects, or even to participatory models, where local people are included in decision-making processes controlled by the aid industry or the state, this project which became an NGO has not been built by outsiders. They emerged, developed, and are widely recognised as a product of favela territories. Activists and leadership were born and/or grew up and continue to live in the favela of Pereirão and this organisation holds a strong territorial link with the specific community of Pereirão. Indeed, territory is central to their identity and their activities.

The authors of *Morrinho* already tried to apply the model of the project to other Brazilian favelas but it did not work because, according to the authors, each favela has its own specific problems and specific cultural references. This shows that even apparently similar communities might show differences and peculiarities and in order to implement a project with success, it is necessary to understand and embed – the real and not what might be assumed to be real – existing cultural references.

A thorough analysis of the theory related to embedding the existing cultural references in projects for social change and practical projects where there was a study and an attempt to integrate the existing cultural references, leads to the conclusion that an analysis, understanding, respect, and integration of cultural references are of utmost importance in such projects. Although, it was observed that there are many levels of engagement in conducting a study of the culture of a community. More significantly, it became clear that it is very difficult to comprehend fully all the cultural references when the project leaders do not share the same references. The project that showed more success in this was *Morrinho* due to its specific characteristic of being created from and to the community. However, this is not to say that it is impossible to create change coming from the outside. On the contrary, *Morrinho* showed that it was also important to build bridges with people outside their community, otherwise the change of perception from the outside would never happen. But it is important to acknowledge that a full understanding and respect of the realities and multiple stories, both from the past (as observed in *Project Row Houses* and in *Morrinho*, where traditions were of utmost importance) and the present is of great importance to integrate the existing cultural references in a project for social change. It is also possible to conclude that acknowledging the differences of cultures is crucial when implementing such a project.

Project management: understanding complexity

In *Intervene: Heroes and Villains*, ideas of project management were applied during the project but not as thoroughly and deeply as its professional meaning warrants. The concept of project manager was mentioned several times in interviews conducted during this research but the phases in the life of the project were not fully understood or applied. It is not that it is always necessary to apply all phases in every project (as noted in The Guide to the PMD Pro, 2013) but it seems that this project lacked a full understanding of the needs of the community and, in particular, a plan for what would happen after the nine-month project ended as the goal was to prevent early-age dropout from school in the long term and not only for the teenagers involved in the nine-month project. From this observation, it seems very important to understand that each project and each organisation is unique, with different goals. In order to meet the goals, it appears to be necessary to adjust the phases of life of the project accordingly and make a realistic plan that does not look only at short-term change but also at what happens next, after the project ends. This corresponds to what The Guide to PM (2013) describes as Project Monitoring, Evaluation and Control; and End of Project Transition. Even though the project followed the traditional life phases of a project, it was very incomplete in terms of project deliverables and project risk management, which could make a great difference in terms of the long-term outcomes that the project has set.

The complexity of *Morrinho* relates to the fact that they are hybrids and seem not to fit into any one single model of NGO, private company, or social movement. They incorporate various elements of all these and do not conform easily to frameworks that juxtapose styles of dealing with and thinking about social transformation. They do not oppose states and markets, nor distance themselves from international agencies and academia, nor separate social movements from these various arenas, but instead work with all in their exhibitions and film productions both for institutions and companies.

In *Morrinho*, though, the authors want so much to protect their rights, as artists, and their identity as a community that they tend to not trust outsiders. They welcome volunteers to help but they do not give them a management, artistic, or leadership role. On the one hand – or, under the lenses of project management – they could, in fact, benefit from an outsider's point of view on their organisation, especially when it comes to planning and fundraising in an effective and organised way, through, for example, an exploration of the six phases of the life of a project (Guide to the PMD Pro, 2011): Project Identification and Design Project Set Up; Project Planning; Project Implementation; Project Monitoring, Evaluation and Control; and End of Project Transition. On the other hand, though, *Morrinho* is – in its own way – successful. They have managed to change the reality of many children in the favela of Pereirão and, on a bigger scale, the young artists have managed to effectively present the favela as a place where conflict, creativity, and citizenship co-exist. In other words, *Morrinho* is presenting an alternative to the (grand) narrative of project management.

Art, cultural studies and project management: overcoming grand narratives

It is not necessarily true that different descriptions, points of view, or disciplines in dialogue can provide solutions for a problem. In fact, the first impulse, despite combining different points of view on the same problem, is to assume that one is better than the other: more accurate, more complete, or preferable on aesthetic, ethical, or political grounds. This assumption forms the condition not only for conflict, but also for progress. While improvement can happen gradually, imagining various ways of experiencing and living, working towards the same aim is the work of revolutionaries – not only in politics, but also in art or even science: "What were ducks in the scientist's world before the revolution are rabbits afterwards" (Kuhn, 1962).

Some common assumptions about the disciplines of art and project management can be found when analysing the links between these disciplines. A common (mistaken) assumption is that art is a discipline praising chaos, creativity, and refusing organisational methods but this is not completely true as chaos is studied by Arts and there are many activities in Arts that show a will to manage within a plan, even though management in this context might mean something different – probably less planned, less monitored, less controlled, more risky, more conflictual, more creative – than it means to a project manager. In the case of project management, this is usually seen as a very structured and balanced discipline but where creativity is not understood. This assumption is wrong as, in modern project management, creativity is regarded as something pivotal to projects. It seems relevant to look at assumptions and preconceived ideas and find ways to clarify them as a means to evolve. Common assumptions might be the reason why art projects claiming to be multidisciplinary are, in fact, multidisciplinary only within creative and similar disciplines. If the assumptions and preconceived ideas about disciplines could be clarified, maybe it would be easier to integrate very different disciplines in the same project in contrast to the fear of different ideas that might, in fact, not be as divergent as they first appear.

Multidisciplinarity within social practice has been positioned "in the areas of spatial practice, artistic research, experimental geography, performance art, dance, and theatre" (Marcellini and Rana, 2012, p. 286). This shows that even though the discipline of art acknowledges the importance of multidisciplinarity, it seems that what is meant by multidisciplinarity through the lens of art is something that could be described more as various creative disciplines together, which is not exactly the same as multidisciplinarity as a combination of varied knowledge.

The theoretical framework of art, cultural studies and project management show that these discourses share concepts such as chaos, creativity, and participation but each one is applied differently by each discipline. Whereas in art, chaos is seen as a way to achieve order, in project management as in other scientific disciplines, chaos is seen in relation to complexity and the goal is to manage chaos. Both disciplines understand the importance of chaos but look at it differently.

The way the concepts of chaos, participation, and creativity are seen and applied may differ according to discipline but there are also points in common. Contemporary art has an interest in incorporating chaos theory, even though the understanding of chaos theory in art is different from the understanding of chaos theory in the disciplines of cultural studies and project management. Combining various views, from the more creative and chaotic to the more analytical and pragmatic, in a multidisciplinary approach, fruitful tensions might come up and lead to conclusions on how to produce effective social change. It seems that we are still far from such multidisciplinary discourse as grand narratives inherent to each disciplinary discourse prevail.

Participation is another concept shared by art and project management: Thamhain compares project managers to a social architect whose major concern should be one of understanding and possibly changing human behaviours through carefully designed projects that seek to involve through participation the members of a population to improve their own communities (2002), an idea mindful of the concept of social sculpture coined by Joseph Beuys. Even though both discourses advocate the importance of participation, both use it in different ways: a project manager as a social architect has a very influential role in the community as he is the one initiating and designing a project; under the concept of social sculpture, in the arts, participation is a trope for social change within any community and any community member is seen equally as an active and creative member with the same role in the community. It is not that one definition is better or more accurate than the other, but it is important to establish a dialogue between them.

Despite the gaps and misunderstandings between the disciplines of art and project management, during the research, it was found that there are links in the Histories of both disciplines and also that there is a growing interest in the link between art and project management, which is especially visible in academic programmes and toolkits for arts and culture.

Furthermore, both disciplines can potentially benefit from a better understanding of each other's characteristics and approaches. Traditionally, project management is bound to control, measurement, monitoring, and evaluation of the planning and execution of a project, its results and the produced knowledge. In the context of innovative projects and projects for social change, the environment is often considered as unstable and dynamic; processes of idea generation are complex and difficult to manage and creativity becomes very important. Even though project management acknowledges the importance of creativity, it also looks for control and it might benefit from integration and combination of its more rational and practical understanding of creativity with the more subjective and free approach of art towards the same concept.

In the research, it was observed that art uses project management in very informal ways in projects with very loose descriptions of the discipline and dismisses any formal level of knowledge. This may lead to a surface application of project management phases in art projects. Even though some art-based projects show an alternative to the grand narrative of project management with their free use of the discipline in the way that it actually works, it is also acknowledged that this implies major risks such as for the sustainability of the project, which sometimes means its evolution into an organisation.

From the study of the possible links between art, cultural studies, and project management, it seems that the most important lessons reside in understanding that one concept might have different meanings from the perspective of different disciplines; and that a multidisciplinary approach benefits from putting together very different disciplines in an understanding and inclusive dialogue, even if this means putting conflicting ideas together. It was observed that art projects tend to claim they are multidisciplinary when they are, in fact, putting together mainly similarly creative and artistic disciplines. Whereas such conflict of ideas is likely to be consensual, confronting truly different disciplines might be tense. But it is precisely in such tensions that something new can arise. In other words, where transformation might occur.

Luhmann's idea of structural couplings (1992) sheds light on the problem found in the current multidisciplinary discourse, which is characterised by grand narratives. Structural couplings describe that different systems may co-evolve over time and systematically communicate about the same themes and within specific contexts, but in their specific and different codes. In other words, each system has its own discourse but each one can communicate about the same ideas keeping their references. Within the same organisational framework, different systems and codes (as well as disciplinary discourses) may learn to co-evolve and also build common institutions despite the distinctive differences. These learning processes seem to lead to a broader, multidisciplinary discourse that could integrate the different views of the same concepts. Such an approach opens the way for new conclusions rather than dismissing what each discipline truly means by the use of each concept.

5   Concluding remarks
Overcoming preconceived ideas in projects for social change

This research began with the observation that art is showing a growing interest in participating and intervening in daily life, in a close relationship with the social realm. This has led to the assumption that art could produce effective social change, an assumption that was rapidly proved partially wrong as art projects seem to dismiss the importance of existing cultural references and how crucial these are to understanding what change is truly needed and how it can be achieved. It was also understood that most art projects lack, on the one hand, a structure with specific aims and goals and, on the other hand, an understanding of what multidisciplinarity entails outside of the artistic realm.

In the observation and description of *Morrinho*, the importance of understanding and integrating the existing cultural references was natural, in contrast to a mediated or imposed process. The project was done by and for the community whereas projects initiated by artists are usually conducted by outsiders who do not hold the complete knowledge, experience, and information of what the community needs and wants. This was precisely the case in *Project Row Houses,* in which it was assumed that by changing the aesthetics of the Third Ward, people would stop fearing to go there and would regard it as a safe place. This was partially true but this was not the main problem of the community; their main problem, as stated by them during the project, was the lack of jobs. The project had then to adapt and find solutions for what was really needed. In the case of *Morrinho*, there was no outsider identifying a problem. The community started the project out of their own needs.

The change in *Morrinho* was possible because of both the natural integration of the existing cultural references within the favela of Pereirão and the self-perception at an individual level. When handing the cameras to the children, the film makers trusted the children, which resulted in their empowerment. This effect was achieved possibly more through the trust than through the participation implied in the act. It was here that the game became a project – children started regarding themselves as artists, changing their self-perception. This shift of self-perception from a child whose self-image was of a criminal and poor to someone who could be seen as an artist, with a job, showed them they could have the power to change the preconceived ideas of what a favela might mean, which became the aim of the project. They make use of art, culture, imagination, and creativity to subvert stereotypes and connect urban spaces, rendering the culture of favelas visible and attractive in the eyes of the city, the country, and the world (through the documentary "God knows everything but is not a snitch", public presentations on the project, and the travelling exhibition of the model of *Morrinho*, including performances). The way the community perceives itself helps in changing preconceived ideas and puts aside fears, contributing to find new ways to develop the surroundings.

This relates to Luhmann's idea of social system: art makes observations of the reality that are also the subject of other observations. Such observations operate in the realm of perception. In *Morrinho*, it was by changing their self-perception that the children changed their own reality along the way, with the creation of a project, which can be understood as a space in the middle of the existing community and reality. Once they changed their self-perception, they changed the ways they communicate the realities they live in: favelados, yes, but in a favela that is not only a space for criminality and fear but also a space filled with stories, where people have jobs and travel the world as in any other place. When presenting this reality, they show a perception that contradicts the grand narrative of the favela.

During the research, one of the main reasons related to the failure of art-based projects emerged from the lack of structure with specific aims and goals that most of these projects show. This takes us to the alternative narrative that *Morrinho* gives to project management, including its approach to chaos, an idea that is understood both by arts and project management but in different ways. *Morrinho* started as a game, without a specific aim and in a chaotic way. Their path, starting from a game and, today, being an NGO, more than a project, shows the approach that arts has towards chaos – chaos as a means to achieve order.

In their own chaotic way, with lack of planning and coherent leadership style that seem to bring problems to the development and concretisation of their activities and also seem to compromise the sustainability of the project, they have managed to survive, despite the problems and struggles they face. In other words, they have managed the project in an alternative way in what might be understood as an alternative narrative to the grand narrative of project from the perspective of project management. In this alternative to the grand narrative of project management, *Morrinho* proves that the shift of perception can lead to social change, even if without a plan, giving room for project management to rethink some of its assumptions towards art and projects, in general.

The grand narratives of disciplines found in the projects analysed as well as when observing the links between different disciplines show that the current multidisciplinary discourse in projects for social change shows a lack of understanding and integration of the existing cultural references both from a community and from each disciplinary discourse. Creative disciplines seem to perceive scientific disciplines as dull whereas these seem to perceive the creative and artistic disciplines as unable to plan.

Perception is very pertinent to *Morrinho*: the project aims to overcome the preconceived ideas (or perceptions) of what a favela might mean. When critically looking at this project, as well as other multidisciplinary projects, through observation, interviews, the understanding of its existing cultural references, and the analysis of the idea of multidisciplinarity, it is striking to see that multidisciplinary projects, with a strong artistic focus, fighting preconceived ideas, show themselves to be preconceived ideas within the disciplines in which they operate and also towards other disciplines that they would rather not include in their discourses.

This conclusion takes us back to the grand narratives that the current multidisciplinary discourse holds. The first possible answer to the problem of inefficacy of artistic projects for social change, proposes that linking and integrating the knowledge of different disciplines in a multidisciplinary approach might be useful in such projects. In this research, Cultural Studies and Project Management emerged as essential disciplines in any project aiming at social change as these projects always imply complexity and cultural issues (assuming that every community, every individual, has cultural references). Art was first assumed as the discipline to be the engine for social change and, even though art alone cannot do much, it shows very important characteristics that can boost the success of a project for social change including creativity, participation, empowerment, and the capacity to perceive the world and show it in various ways. It was precisely when multidisciplinarity was seen as a possible solution for projects for social change, that the grand narratives to each disciplinary discourse were found and multidisciplinarity became both the solution and the problem.

Participation is important for art but also for cultural studies and project management as was seen in the theoretical framework. Nevertheless, the way the disciplines use the same idea is different. When artists ask people for participation in building a social organism for a better society (as in the social sculpture advocated by Beuys), the approach lies in free participation, without assigned roles or specific aims, putting the focus on the freedom of the individual. As for project management, participation is important but under control and planning. None seems to be completely right as history shows many projects failing in both areas and a possible solution would be the understanding and combination of both approaches in a balanced way.

Whereas art seems to fear that scientific disciplines, as project management, might take away the creative spark of a project, it also seems that scientific disciplines look at art as a discipline incapable of dealing with specific goals and timings and within a formal plan in tasks that need thorough analysis and planning. This study shows that these are wrong assumptions and that each discipline has a strong tendency to be naive about the rest of the world.

At first sight, the proposal of combining and integrating such apparently different disciplines might sound odd. Art and science appear as opposites as science is usually connected with rationality and methodology whereas art is usually associated with subjectivity and chaos. Despite the misunderstandings or assumptions, there is a mutual fascination between arts and science – many artists work with engineers or within an engineering concept (we can go as far back as Leonardo da Vinci's detailed plans of flying machines) and science is about discovery, which implies creativity.

Whereas art is usually regarded as chaotic, scientific disciplines such as project management are usually seen as anti-creative. These are common assumptions that show how each disciplinary discourse has grand narratives attached. If we look at contemporary art and the field of arts management there is a contradiction to this grand narrative as there is a clear need and will to work within organisational, communication, and management parameters. In recent history of art, there is a need to embed the characteristics and methods of scientific disciplines, with a strong focus on project management. This is seen in various ways: from public art projects and museums hiring art project managers, to art projects for social change claiming to use project management in their methods, and in the creation of academic courses relating to art and project management. This might be due to the change of needs in art history with the creation of complex programmes ranging from art biennales with many artists and international organisations as well as educational activities where there is a need to plan what to do and for whom, with a clear understanding of the public.

Project management can therefore be considered as one of the fundamentals of the successful management of the creative sector; crucial to the long-term sustainability of arts and culture and ensuring a sound and stable environment in which artists can be creative. In a reciprocal relationship, businesses, policy makers, and academics have consistently made the case for the importance of creative disciplines such as art and design as tools for innovation, productivity, and economic growth and, therefore, social change or improvement. Many have argued that art is a link between creativity and innovation. This relates to the idea of creative capital claimed by Joseph Beuys according to which creativity is not only the domain of artists as capital is not only the domain of science and management. His assumption proves to be a milestone for a broader multidisciplinary discourse where the concepts are not exclusive to any specific discipline. This implies that each discipline has its own use and view of different concepts in contrast to the idea that an artist would never be able to plan and work with capital or that a project manager is unable to think in a creative way.

One concept that has different readings by science and art is chaos. Chaos theory is usually connected to science but it is also studied by arts. Whereas in art, chaos is seen as a way to achieve order, in project management as in other scientific disciplines, chaos is seen in relation to complexity and the goal is to manage chaos. In a way, both art and scientific disciplines, as project management, are looking to find order through chaos. In art, chaos theory explores the impossibility of predicting what comes next and the exponential amplification of errors or lapses of memory. Chaos in a dynamic project management system can be defined as an unpredictable or disorderly event;

an event that renews and revitalises the process; small changes in initial conditions leading to enormous consequences; similar patterns that take place across layers (fractal geometry); decisions that need to be made even in the absence of all intended information.

The inspiration that art takes from the scientific domain is clear but sticks to only one of the characteristics of the Theory and seems to dismiss the depth of the complexity involved in chaos theory. It is an interpretation and it is interesting to observe that there are many attempts at integration of scientific theories in art but it is also important to acknowledge that these types of differences in meaning and perception lead to misunderstandings between different disciplinary discourses.

Another grand narrative is that project management is usually known as a discipline dismissing creativity. In modern project management, creativity is highly regarded, which contradicts this assumption. Project management has consistently stated and defended the importance of creative disciplines as art and design as tools for innovation, productivity, and economic growth and, therefore, social change or improvement.

There are some concepts in common in arts, cultural studies, and project management, such as chaos, creativity, and participation. The way the same concepts are viewed in each discipline shows, nevertheless, various differences. This might be one of the reasons why the combination of the scientific disciplines and art is still rather problematic and needs further study. The concluding remark lies exactly in this need for further study in the combination and integration of the different ideas towards the same concepts by each discipline. Each discipline shows its specific narratives towards social change but, alone, each of them shows problems in being successful.

Finally, and this is the last issue to be touched upon here, it is possible to observe that the lessons learned point to a possible conclusion of this study, which remains open for future research focusing on the importance of structuring the interface between the histories of the different disciplines and the alternative narratives that can be observed in this disciplinary terrain.

The proposal of this research is that combining and integrating the characteristics and knowledge of art (as creativity, participation, and empowerment) with cultural studies (in its material and immaterial relations to society) and project management (as it structures the project – it could be seen as the skeleton of a project as it is essential for keeping its balance through all phases) might increase the success of a project. Multidisciplinarity is proposed as the approach to combine these disciplines as it implies their combination and integration, in a balanced and horizontal, non-hierarchical process, in different phases.

Nevertheless, one of the conclusions about the role of multidisciplinarity in linking art, cultural studies, and project management in projects for social change is the current rejection of analysing common assumptions and preconceived ideas and finding ways to clarify it as a means to evolve. Common assumptions and preconceived ideas about what each discipline might encompass may be the reason why art projects claiming to be multi-disciplinary are, in fact, multidisciplinary only within creative and similar disciplines. If the assumptions and preconceived ideas about disciplines and their different notions about the same concepts could be clarified, it would be easier to integrate very different disciplines in the same project, in a broader and more inclusive multidisciplinary discourse.

The final conclusion resides in understanding that the current multidisciplinary discourse holds grand narratives and the solution lies in finding a broader multidisciplinary discourse. Suggestions for future research lie in looking at the histories of each discipline and understanding if, where, and why there are points in common. By going back to the history of each discipline it might be possible to understand both weaknesses and strengths in their historical evolution and alternative narratives to each discipline might be found in the histories of apparently very different disciplines.

Comprehension and integration of the actual meanings – as opposed to biased ideas – of each discipline will, possibly, lead to results for the accomplishment of projects for effective social change. As the research shows, we are still far from a broader discourse of multidisciplinarity – each discipline has a strong tendency to be naive about the rest of the world. Such broadening will allow for productive and true integration and collaboration between disciplines that, isolated, cannot develop successful projects aiming at social change. If the aim is actual social change, a broader multidisciplinary approach is needed, as the research shows.

This multidisciplinary approach understands the importance of not only looking thoroughly into the histories and true meanings of each discipline but also of planning and strategic thinking without dismissing creativity and the power of the individual.

What this research tells us is that grand narratives are inherently cultural constructs that affect different levels of society as well as disciplinary discourses acting upon it. The role of art in unveiling these grand narratives is inherently conflictual as it involves rupture and the collision of differences as methodologies to perceive, reflect upon, and visually translate (alternative proposals to) the grand narratives that seem to make the world we live in. It is precisely this type of conflict in combining different disciplinary discourses that is crucial in projects for social change. To defy the limits of structural changes in a progressive way implies an ethical and critical work, both free and within the system that presupposes figures reclaiming their right of acting as strategists and mediators. The understanding and recognition of these figures and their strategies is essential to develop the creative and changing potential of new narratives in a contemporary, conflicting society. If we want, either as citizens, artists, cultural agents, or project managers, to join this endeavour of creating new strategies and challenging the world we live in – here and now – it is our entire responsibility.

Bibliography

Abbasi, G. Y. and Al-Mharmah, H. A. (2000). Project management practice by the public sector in a developing country. *International Journal of Project Management* (18), 105–109.

Adorno, T. W. (1958). *Aesthetic Theory.* (C. Lenhardt, trans.) London: Routledge and Kegan Paul.

Allison, M. (2002). Into the fire: boards and executive transitions. *Non-profit Management & Leadership*(12), 341–351.

Álvarez, S. E., Dagnino, E., and Escobar, A. (1998). The Cultural and the Political in Latin American Social Movements. In S. E. Álvarez, E. Dagnino and A. Escobar (eds.), *Cultures of Politics, Politics of Culture: Re-visioning Latin American Social Movements.* Boulder, CO: Westview Press, pp. 1–29.

Anbari, F. T., Khilkhanova, E., Romanova, M., and Umpleby, S. (2004). Managing cultural differences in international projects. *Journal of International Business and Economics* (2), 267–274.

Andrulis, D. P., Siddiqui, N. J., and Purtle, J. (2011, February). Guidance for integrating culturally diverse communities into planning for and responding to emergencies: a toolkit. Retrieved January 19, 2013 from www.hhs.gov/ocr/civilrights/resources/specialtopics/emergencypre/omh_diversitytoolkit.pdf.

Arnaboldi, M., Azzone, G., and Savoldelli, A. (2004). Managing a public sector project: the case of the Italian Treasury Ministry. *International Journal of Project Management* (22), 213–223.

Arrow, K. J. (1974). *The Limits of Organization.* New York: W. W. Norton & Company.

Augé, M. (1995). *Non-Places: Introduction to an Anthropology of Supermodernity.* (J. Howe, trans.) London and NY: Verso.

Barrett, R. (2003). *Vocational Business: Training, Developing and Motivating People.* Cheltenham: Nelson Thornes.

Barthes, R. (1977). *Introduction to the Structuralist Analysis of Narratives.* New York: Hill and Wang.

Baskerville, R. F. (2005). A research note: The unfinished business of culture. Retrieved January 10, 2012 from SSRN: http://ssrn.com/abstract=1208874.

Baum, H. S. (1997). *The Organization of Hope: Communities Planning Themselves.* Albany, NY: State University of New York.

Baumol, W. and Benhabib, J. (1989). Chaos: significance, mechanism, and economic applications. *Journal of Economic Perspectives* (3), pp. 77–105.

Bertelsen, S. (2002). *Complexity – Construction in a New Perspective.* Gramado: IGLC.

Bertelsen, S. and Koskela, L. (2003). Avoiding and managing chaos in projects. In: *Proceedings of the 11th annual conference of the International Group for Lean Construction*, 22-24 July. Blacksburg, VA: Virginia Tech.

Bishop, C. (2004). Antagonism and Relational Aesthetics. *October Magazine* (110), 51–79.

Bishop, C. (2006, February). The social turn: collaboration and its discontents. *Arforum*, 178–185.

Blom, I. (2007). *On the Style Site Art, Sociality, and Media Culture.* Berlin: Sternberg Press.

Boal, A. (1992). *Games for Actors and Non-Actors.* London: Routledge.

Boje, D. (1991). Organizations as storytelling networks: a study of story performance in an office-supply firm. *Administrative Science Quarterly*, 106–126.

Boje, D. (1995). Stories of the storytelling organization: a postmodern analysis of Disney as Tamara-land. *Academy of Management Journal* 38(4), 997–1035.

Boje, D. M. (2007). The Antenarrative Cultural Turn in Narrative Studies. In M. Zachry and C. Thralls (eds.), *Communicative Practices in Workplaces and the Professions: Cultural Perspectives on the Regulation of Discourse and Organizations.* Amityville, NY: Baywood Publishing.

Bonami, F. (2005, January 1). The legacy of a myth maker. *Tate Etc* (3), 5–8.

Bott, E. (1957). *Family and Social Networks.* London: Tavistock.

Bourdieu, P. (1984). *Distinction: A Social Critique of the Judgement of Taste.* Cambridge: Harvard University Press.

Bourdieu, P. and Darbel, A. (1969). *The Love of Art: European Art Museums and their Public.* (C. Beattie and N. Merriman, trans.) Cambridge, UK: Polity Press.

Bourriaud, N. (1998). *Relational Aesthetics.* Dijon: Les presses du réel.

Boyce, M. E. (1995). Collective centring and collective sense-making in the stories and storytelling of one organization. *Organization Studies* 16(1), 107–137.

Brecht, B. (1930/1983) Radio as a Means of Communication. In A. Mattelart and S. Siegelaub (eds.), *Communication and Class Struggle 2: Liberation, Socialism.* New York: International General.

Breton, A. and Rivera, D. (1938). *Manifesto for an Independent Revolutionary Art.* Free Rein. Lincoln: Nebraska UP, 1996. 29–34.

British Design Council. (2010). *Multidisciplinary Design Education in the UK.* London: British Design Council.

Butler, A. (1990). A methodological missing approach to chaos: are economists the point? *Federal Reserve Bank of St. Louis Review* 72(2), 36–48.

Carayannis, E. G., Kwak, Y.-H., and Anbari, F. T. (2005). *The Story of Managing Projects: An Interdisciplinary Approach.* Westport, Connecticut: Greenwood Publishing Group.

Carroll, G. and Hannan, M. (2004). *The Demography of Corporations and Industries.* Princeton, NJ: Princeton University Press.

Cartwright, T. J. (1991). Planning and chaos theory. *Journal of the American Planning Association* (57), 44–56.

Castoriadis, C. (1987). *The Imaginary Institution of Society.* Cambridge: Polity.

Centre for Contemporary Cultural Studies. (1980a). *On Ideology.* London: Hutchinson.

Centre for Contemporary Cultural Studies. (1980b). *Culture, Media, Language.* London: Hutchinson.

Chabota, M. and Duhaimea, G. (1998). Land-use planning and participation: the case of inuit public housing (Nunavik, Canada). *Habitat International* (22), 429–447.

Cleaver, F. (1999). Paradoxes of participation: questioning participatory approaches to development. *Journal of International Development* (11), 597–612.

Cohendet, P. and Simon, L. (2007). Playing across the playground: paradoxes of knowledge creation in the video-game firm. *Journal of Organizational Behavior* (28), 587–605.

Corsi, G., Sposito, E., and Baraldi, C. (1996). *Glosario sobre la Teoría Social de Niklas Luhmann.* México: Universidad Ibero Americana, Iteso, Editorial Antrophos.

Cremer, H.and GahvariF. (1993). Tax evasion and optimal commodity taxation. *Journal of Public Economics* (50), 261–275.

Crimmin, M. and Stanton, E. (eds.) (2014). *Art and Conflict.* London: Royal College of Art, p. 5.

Cullmann, S. (2013, August). Creativity and project management: managing the unexpected and permanent change. *Journal of Modern Project Management,* 87–101.

Dean, J. (2000). Introduction: The Interface of Political Theory and Cultural Studies. In J. Dean (ed.), *Cultural Studies and Political Theory.* Ithaca and London: Cornell University Press, p. 5.

Delanty, G. (2000). *Citizenship in a Global Age: Society, Culture, Politics.* Buckingham: Open University Press.

Deleuze, G. and Guattari, F. (1994). *What is Philosophy?*New York: Columbia University Press.

Deutsch, K. W.et al. (1957). *Political Community and the North Atlantic Area.* Princeton, NJ: Princeton University Press.

Dewey, J. (1933). *How We Think.* New York: Prometheus Books.

Diaz-Albertini, J. (1993). Non-profit advocacy in weakly institutionalised political systems: the case of NGDOs in Lima, Peru. *Non-profit and Voluntary Sector Quarterly* (27), 317–337.

Elmes, M. and Wilemon, D. (1988). Organizational Culture and Project Leader Effectiveness. *Project Management Journal* (19), pp. 54–63.

Entman, R. M. (1990). Modern racism and the images of blacks in local television news. *Critical Studies in Mass Communication,* 7(4), 332–345. doi:10.1080/15295039009360183.

FayolH. (1916/1949). *General and Industrial Management.* London: Sir Isaac Pitman & Sons, Ltd.

Fiske, J. (1989a). *Understanding Popular Culture.* London:Routledge.

Fiske, J. (1989b). *Reading the Popular.* London: Unwin Hyman Ltd.

Foster, H. (2015). *Bad New Days: Art, Criticism, Emergency.* London: Verso.

Fricke, H. (2000). "The World marked as ready-made". In C. Esche (ed.), *Amateur.* Göteborg: Göteborg Art Museum.

Fries, S. (n/d). Cultural, multicultural, cross-cultural, intercultural: a moderator's proposal. Retrieved March 10, 2013 from Tesol France: www.tesol-france.org/articles/fries.pdf.

Fuchs, C. (2018). Research paper INTAS project. Human Strategies in Complexity #4.

Fuchs, C. and Holzner, F. (2005). Art as a Complex Dynamic System. Social Science Research Network e-Library, SSRN.

Garber, M. (2001). *Academic Instincts.* Princeton and London: Princeton University Press.

Garcia, S. (1993). *Europe and the Search for Identity.* London: Pinter.

Gibson, A. (1996). *Towards a Postmodern Theory of Narrative.* Edinburgh: Edinburgh University Press.

Gilson, L., Palmer, N., and Schneider, H. (2005). Trust and health worker performance: exploring a conceptual framework using South African evidence. *Social Science and Medicine* (61), 1418–1429.

Goldberger, A. L., Rigney, D. R., and West, B. J. (1990). Chaos and fractals in physiology. *Scientific American* (263), 43–49.

Griffin, E. (2012). *A First Look at Communication Theory* (8th ed.). New York: The McGraw-Hill Companies, Inc.

Groys, B.(2009, December 11). Comrades of time. *e-flux journal.*

Guggenheim Museum (2008). theanyspacewhatever. Retrieved April 29, 2013 from Guggenheim Museum: http://web.guggenheim.org/exhibitions/anyspace/exhibition.html.

Haas, E. B. (1958). *The Uniting of Europe.* Stanford: Stanford University Press.

Hailey, J. (2001). Beyond the Formulaic: Process and Practice in South Asian NGOs. In B. Cooke and U. Kothari (eds.), *Participation: The New Tyranny?*London: Zed Books, pp. 88–101.

Hailey, J. and James, R. (2004). Trees die from the top: international perspectives on NGO leadership development. *Voluntas* 15(4), 345–353.

Hall, S., Jefferson, T., and University of Birmingham, Centre for Contemporary Cultural Studies (1976). *Resistance Through Rituals: Youth Subcultures in Post-war Britain.* London: Hutchinson.

Harrison, R. (1974). In B. Rosamond, *Theories of European Integration.* Houndmills: Palgrave.

Hassard, J. (1993). Postmodernism and Organizational Analysis. In J. H. Parker, *Postmodernism and Organizations.* London: Sage, pp. 1–23.

Hatchuel, A., Masson, P. L., and Weil, B. (2011, January). Teaching innovative design reasoning: how C-K theory can help to overcome fixation effect. *Artificial Intelligence for Engineering Design. Analysis and Manufacturing* (25), 77–92.

Heath, C. and Sitkin, S. (2001). Big-B versus Big-O: what is organizational about organizational behavior? *Journal of Organizational Behavior* (22), 53–58.

Henrie, M. and Sousa-Poza, A. (2005). Project management: a cultural literary review. *Project Management Journal* (36), 5–14.

Hofstede, G. (1991). *Cultures and Organizations: Software of the Mind.* London: McGraw-Hill.

Hofstede, G. (2003). Culture's consequences: comparing values, behaviors, institutions, and organizations across nations. *Behaviour Research and Therapy* (41), 861–862.

Houghton, S. A., Furumura, Y., Lebedko, M., and Li, S. (2013). *Critical Cultural Awareness: Managing Stereotypes through Intercultural (Language) Education.* Newcastle upon Tyne, UK: Cambridge Scholars Publishing.

Huber, G. and Glick, W. (1993). Sources and Forms of Organizational Change. In G. Huber and W. Glick (eds.), *Organizational Change and Redesign: Ideas and Insights for Improving Performance.* Oxford: Oxford University Press.

Jackson, M. C. (2003). The Origins and Nature of Critical Systems Thinking. In Midgley, G. (ed.), *Systems Thinking* (Vol. 4, pp. 227–253). London: Sage.

Jackson, T. and Sorgenfrei, M. (2003) *The PraxisNote N°1 - How Can Knowledge Transferability Be Managed Across Cultures?*Oxford:INTRAC.

Javidan, M., House, R. J., Dorfman, P. W., Hanges, P. J., and Luque, S. D. (2006). Conceptualizing and measuring cultures and their consequences: a comparative review of GLOBE's and Hofstede's approaches. *Journal of International Business Studies* (37), 897–914.

Johnson, R., Chambers, D., Raghuram, P., and Tincknell, E. (2004). *The Practice of Cultural Studies*. London: Sage.

Jovchelovitch, S. and Hérnandez, J. P. (2012). *Underground Sociabilities: Identity, Culture and Resistance in Rio de Janeiro's Favelas*. London: London School of Economics.

Kanpol, B. and Mclaren, P. (1995). *Critical Multiculturalism: Uncommon Voices in a Common Struggle*. Westport, Connecticut: Praeger.

Kellner, D. (1995). *Media Culture. Cultural Studies, Identity, and Politics Between the Modern and the Postmodern*. London and New York: Routledge.

Kellner, D. (1997). Overcoming the Divide: Cultural Studies and Political Economy. In M. Ferguson and P. Golding (eds.), *Cultural Studies in Question*. London: Sage, pp. 102–119.

Kellner, D. (1998). Cultural studies and social theory: a critical intervention. Retrieved January 6, 2014 from Graduate School of Education and Information Studies Faculty and Staff Pages: www.gseis.ucla.edu/faculty/kellner/kellner.html.

Kelsey, D. (1988). The economics of chaos or the chaos of economics. *Oxford Economic Papers* (40), 1–31.

Kerzner, H. (1998). *Project Management: A System Approach to Planning, Scheduling, and Controlling*. New York: John Wiley and Sons.

Kerzner, H. (2004). *Advanced Project Management: Best Practices on Implementation*. Somerset: Wiley.

Kiel, D. and Elliott, E. (1996). *Chaos Theory and Social Sciences*. Michigan: University of Michigan Press.

Klein, Louis (2011/2012). White Paper – social complexity in project management. Retrieved February 13, 2013 from Systemic Excellence Group: www.systemic-excellence-group.com/sites/default/files/121023%20Social%20Complexity%20in%20Project%20Management_0.pdf.

Kliem, R. L. (2004, Summer). Managing the risks of offshore IT development projects. *Information Systems Management Journal*, 22–28.

Klineberg, O. (1964). *The Human Dimension in Interpersonal Relations*. New York: Holt, Rine Hart and Winston.

Klopf, D. W. and Park, M. (1982). *Cross Cultural Communication: An Introduction to the Fundamentals*. Seoul: Hanshin Publishing Co.

Kniffen, F. B. (1936, December). Louisiana house types. *Annals of the Association of American Geographers* (91), 11–13.

Kroeber, A. L. and Kluckhohn, C. (1952). *Culture: A Critical Review of Concepts and Definitions*. Cambridge, MA: Peabody Museum of American Archæology and Ethnology, Harvard University.

Kuhn, T. (1962). *The Structure of Scientific Revolutions*. Chicago: University of Chicago Press.

Kuoni, C. (1990). *Energy Plan for the Western Man: Joseph Beuys in America*. New York: Four Walls Eight Windows.

Larssen, L. B. (2012, January). The long nineties: revisiting art's social turn and the 1990s – the decade that has yet to end. *Frieze* (144), 12–17.

Lash, S. (2007). Power after hegemony: cultural studies in mutation? *Theory, Culture, and Society* (24), 55–78.

Lawrence, R. and Després, C. R. (2004). Introduction: futures of transdisciplinarity. *Futures* (36), 398.

Lewis, D. (2003). Theorising the organisation and management of non-governmental development organisations: towards a composite approach. *Public Management Review* 5(3), 325–344.

Lima, M. A. (1996). *Marginália*. Rio de Janeiro: Salamandra.

Lind, M. (2011). Returning on Bikes: Notes on Social Practice. In N. Thomson (ed.), *Living as Form: Socially Engaged Art from 1991–2011*. New York: The MIT Press, pp. 46–56.

Lindberg, L. N. and Scheingold, S. A. (1971). *Regional Integration: Theory and Research*. Cambridge: Harvard University Press.

Lowe, R. (2012). Project Row Houses – interview with Rick Lowe. In Santos, L. (ed.), *There is No Knife Without Roses*. Stockholm: Tensta Konsthall and Konstfack.

Luhmann, N. (1984). *Soziale Systeme: Grundriß einer allgemeinen Theorie*. Berlin: Suhrkamp Verlag AG.

Luhmann, N. (1990). World Art. In Baecker, N. L. (ed.), *Unobservable World of Art and Architecture*. Bielefeld: Haux, pp. 7–46.

Luhmann, N. (1992). The concept of society. *Thesis Eleven* 31(1), 67–80. https://doi.org/10.1177/072551369203100106.

Luhmann, N. (1993). *Das Recht der Gesellschaft*. Frankfurt: Suhrkamp. English translation: *Law as a Social System*, Oxford: Oxford University Press, 2004.

Luhmann, N. (1995). *Die Kunst der Gesellschaft*. Frankfurt: Suhrkamp. English translation: Art as a Social System, Stanford: Stanford University Press, 2000.

Lukács, G. (1954). *Art and Objective Truth*. London: Merlin.

Malchiodi, C. (2007). *The Art Therapy Sourcebook* (2nd ed.). New York: McGraw Hill.

Manacorda, F. (2013). *Art Turning Left: How Values Changed Making 1789–2013*. London: Tate.

Marcellini, A. and Rana, M. D. (2012). Notes toward a non-anthropocentric social practice. *Paletten Art Journal*, 286–287.

Marcuse, H. (1978). *The Aesthetic Dimension: Toward a Critique of Marxist Aesthetics*. Boston: Beacon Press.

Marinetti, F. T. (1909) The Futurist Manifesto. First published in *Le Figaro*, 20 Febr. 1909. Transl. James Joll (*Intellectuals in Politics; Three Biographical Essays*. London: Weidenfeld & Nicolson, 1960). Available online at cscs.umich.edu/~crshalizi/T4PM/futurist-manifesto.html.

Marxists Internet Archive (1999–2008). *MIA: Encyclopedia of Marxism*. (A. Blunden, Editor) Retrieved February 13, 2012 from Marxists Internet Archive: www.marxists.org/glossary/terms/c/o.htm#communism.

Marxists.org. *Karl Marx, 1859, A Contribution to the Critique of Political Economy*. Retrieved March 29, 2018 from Marx.org 1993 (Preface, 1993), Marxists.org 1999: www.marxists.org/archive/marx/works/1859/critique-pol-economy/index.htm.

Mayer-Kress, G. and Grossman, S. (1989). Chaos in the international arms race. *Nature* (337), 701–704.

McAdam, D. (1994). *Culture and Social Movements. From New Social Movements: From Ideology to Identity*. Philadelphia: Temple University Press.

McGuigan, J. (1992). *Cultural Populism*. London and New York: Routledge.

McGuigan, J. (1997). *Cultural Methodologies*. NY: Sage.

McSweeney, B. (2002). Hofstede's model of national cultural differences and their consequences: a triumph of faith – a failure of analysis. *Human Relations* (55), 89–118.

Melucci, A. (1980). The new social movements: a theoretical approach. *Social Science Information* 19(2), 199–226.

Merry, U. (1995). *Coping with Uncertainty: Insights from the New Sciences of Chaos, Self-Organization, and Complexity.* Westport, Connecticut: Praeger.

Midler, C. and Lenfle, S. (2003). Gestion de Projet et Innovation. In P. Mustar and H. Penan, *L'Encyclopédie de l'Innovation* (pp. 49–69). Paris: Economica.

Miles, R. E. (1975). *Theories of Management: Implications for Organizational Behaviour and Development.* New York: McGraw-Hill Education.

Mochal, T. and Mochal, J. (2003). *Lessons in Project Management.* Miami, FL: San Val, Incorporated.

Moore, A. (2009). A brief genealogy of social sculpture. Retrieved January 10, 2013 from *The Journal of Aesthetics and Protest.* www.joaap.org/webonly/moore.htm.

Morrinho. (2000). Morrinho, uma pequena revolução. Retrieved December 10, 2011 from Morrinho, uma pequena revolução: www.morrinho.com.

Muriithi, N. and Crawford, L. (2003). Approaches to project management in Africa: implications for international development projects. *International Journal of Project Management* (21), 9–319.

Newman, K. and Nollen, S. D. (1996) Culture and Congruence: The Fit Between Management Practices and National Culture". *Journal of International Business Studies* 27(4), 753–779. https://doi.org/10.1057/palgrave.jibs.8490152.

Nguyen, T. H., Sherif, J. S., and Newby, M. (2007). Strategies for successful CRM implementation . *Journal of Information Management and Computer Security*, 15(2), pp. 102–115.

Nicolescu, B. (1998). The transdisciplinary evolution of learning. Retrieved October 30, 2013 from Learning Development Institute:www.learndev.org/dl/nicolescu_f.pdf.

O'Neill, P. and Wilson, M. (2010) *Curating and the Educational Turn.* London: Open Editions.

Parker, B. (1998). *Globalization and Business Practice: Managing across Boundaries.* London: Sage.

Patel, B. M. (2008). *Project Management: Strategic Financial Planning, Evaluation and Control.* New Delhi: Vikas Publishing House PVT Ltd.

Perlman, J. (1977). *O Mito da Marginalidade: favelas e política no Rio de Janeiro.* Rio de Janeiro: Paz e Terra.

Pettigrew, A. M. (1985). *The Awakening Giant: Continuity and Change at ICI.* Oxford, UK: Basil Blackwell.

Pettigrew, A. M. (1990). Longitudinal field research on change: theory and practice. *Organisation Science* 1(3), 267–292.

Pettigrew, A. M., Woodman, R. W., and Cameron, K. S. (2001). Studying organizational change and development: challenges for future research. *Academy of Management Journal* 44(4), 607–713.

Pinto, J. (2007). *Project Management: Achieving Competitive Advantage.* Upper Saddle River: Pearson Education.

PM4NGOs. (2013, April). PMD Pro guide. Retrieved May 2, 2013 from PM4NGOs: www.pm4ngos.org/index.php/introduction.

PMI (1996). *PMBOK – Project Management Body of Knowledge.* Newton Square, Pennsylvania USA: PMI.

Polkinghorne, D. (1988). *Narrative Knowing and the Human Sciences.* Albany, NY: State University of New York Press.

Porush, D. S. (1993). Making Chaos: Two Views of a New Science. In McRae, M. W. (ed.), *The Literature of Science: Perspectives on Popular Scientific Writing*. Athens: University of Georgia Press, pp. 152–167.

Project Management Institute (PMI). (2013). About us: what is project management. Retrieved March 27, 2013 from Project Management Institute (PMI): www.pmi.org/About-Us/About-Us-What-is-Project-Management.aspx.

Radzicki, M. J. (1990). Institutional dynamics, deterministic chaos, and self-organizing systems. *Journal of Economic Issues* (24), 57–102.

Ramos, S.(2007). Jovens de Favelas na Produção Cultural Brasileira dos anos 90. InM. I.Almeida and S. C. Naves, *Por que não? Rupturas e Continuidades da Contracultura*. Rio de Janeiro: 7Letras. pp. 239–256.

Rhön, D. P. and Whitelaw, G. (2000). Sustainability through transdisciplinarity? In Häberli, R. *Transdisciplinarity: Joint Problem-solving Among Science, Technology and Society. Workbook I: Dialogue sessions and idea market*. Zurich: Haffmans Sachbuch Verlag AG, pp. 425–430.

Rogoff, I. (2008). Turning. *e-flux journal* #0, November 2008, available at www.e-flux.com/journal/00/68470/turning/, last accessed in January 2017.

Rogoff, I. (2010a). Education actualized – editorial. *e-flux journal* #14, March 2010, available at www.e-flux.com/journal/14/61300/education-actualized-editorial/, last accessed in January 2017.

Rogoff, I. (2010b). Free. *e-flux journal* #14, March 2010, available at www.e-flux.com/journal/14/61311/free, last accessed in June 2017.

Rogoff, I. (2013). The Expanded Field. In J.-P. Martinon (ed.), *The Curatorial: A Philosophy of Curating*. London: Bloomsbury, pp. 41–48.

Rowlands, J. (1997). *Questioning Empowerment: Working with Women in Honduras*. Oxford, UK: Oxfam.

Scheringer, J., Jaeger, J., and Esfeld, M. (2000). Transdisciplinarity and Holism. In R. Häberli (ed.), *Transdisciplinarity: Joint Problem-solving Among Science, Technology and Society. Workbook I: Dialogue sessions and idea market*. Zurich: Haffmans Sachbuch Verlag AG, pp. 35–37.

Scheyvens, R. (1999). "Ecotourism and the empowerment of local communities". *Tourism Manager*, 2(20), 245–249.

Schleslinger, P. (1994). Europe as a New Battlefield? In J. H. Smith (ed.), *Nationalism*. Oxford: Oxford University Press.

Serra, C. and Oliveira, C. (2012). Project Morrinho: interview. In L. Santos (ed.), *There is No Knife Without Roses*. Stockholm: Tensta Konsthall and Konstfack.

Silva, Alves da (2003) *Amadora – Um pouco de história. Do outro lado da linha*. Amadora: Centro Social do Bairro 6 de Maio.

Smith, A. (1995). *Nations and Nationalism in a Global Era*. Cambridge: Polity.

Snyder, J. R. and Kline, S. (1987, March). Modern project management: how did we get here – where do we go? *Project Management Journal* 5(1), 2–64.

Sommer, D. (2006). *Cultural Agency in the Americas*. Durham, NC: Duke University Press.

Soysal, Y. (2002). Locating Europe. *European Societies* 4(3): 265–284.

Storr, R. (2007). *Think With the Senses, Feel With the Mind: Art in the Present Tense*. Venice: Marsilio Editions.

Stretton, A. (1994). A short history of project management. Part one: the 1950s and 60s. *The Australian Project Manager* (14), 36–37.

Stromquist, N. (2002). *Education in a Globalized World: The Connectivity of Economic Power, Technology, and Knowledge*. Oxford, UK: Rowman and Littlefield Publishers, Inc.

Thamhain, H. J. (2002). From the special issue guest editor. *Engineer Management Journal* 1, 2–3.

Ting-Toomey, S. (1999). *Communicating Across Cultures*. New York: Guilford Press.

Towen, A. (1996). *Gender and Development in Zambia. Empowerment of Women Through Local Non-governmental Organisations*. Groningen: University of Groningen.

Trompenaars, F. and Hampden-Turner, C. (1998). *Riding the Waves of Culture: Understanding Cultural Diversity in Global Business*. New York: McGraw Hill.

Tucker, S. G. (1995). Re-innovating the African-American Shotgun House [Roots]. *Places* (10), pp. 64–71.

UN-HABITAT(2003). *The Challenge of Slums – Global Report on Human Settlements 2003*. UN-Habitat.

UNESCO (1977). Records of the General Conference Nineteenth Session Nairobi. General Conference Nineteenth Session, Nairobi, 26 October to 30 November 1976. Paris: UNESCO.

UNESCO (1982). World Conference on Cultural Policies – MONDIACULT, México. México: UNESCO.

UNESCO (2001). UNESCO – Building peace in the minds of men and women. Retrieved January 3, 2012 from Universal Declaration on Cultural Diversity: http://portal.unesco.org/en/ev.php-URL_ID=13179&URL_DO=DO_TOPIC&URL_SECTION=201.html.

UNESCO (2011). The cultural diversity lens: A practical tool to integrate culture in development – Pedagogical guide. Retrieved January 3, 2013 from UNESCO – Building peace in the minds of men and women: www.unesco.org/new/fileadmin/MULTIMEDIA/HQ/CLT/pdf/The%20Cultural%20Diversity%20Lens_Pedagogical%20guide.pdf.

UNESCO (2012). New research about favelas is launched during international seminar in Rio de Janeiro. Retrieved October 24, 2013 from UNESCO: www.unesco.org/new/en/brasilia/about-this-office/single-view/news/new_research_about_slums_to_be_launched_during_international_seminar_in_rio_de_janeiro/#.UmkT55QmmCJ.

Upton, D. and Vlach, J. M. (1986). *Common Places*. Georgia: University of Georgia Press.

Valladares, L. (2009). *Social Sciences Representations of Favelas in Rio de Janeiro: A Historical Perspective*. Lille: Lanic Etext Collection.

Valladares, L. D. and Medeiros, L. (2003). *Pensando as favelas do Rio de Janeiro, 1906–2000*. Rio de Janeiro: URBANDATA-Brasil, Relume Dumará.

Velho, G. and Alvito, M. (1996). *Cidadania e Violência*. Rio de Janeiro: Editora UFRJ/Editora FGV.

Ven De Van, A. and Poole, M. S. (1995). Explaining development and change in organizations. *Academy of Management Review* 20(3), 510–540.

Vianna, H. (2001). Não quero que a vida me faça de otário! Hélio Oiticica como mediador cultural entre o asfalto e o morro. In Velho, G. and Kuschnir, K. (eds.) *Mediação, Cultura e Politica*. Rio de Janeiro: Altiplano.

Vlach, J. M. (1976). The Shotgun House: An African Architectural Legacy. In Upton, D. and Vlach, J. M. (eds.) *Common Places: Readings in American Vernacular Architecture*. Athens, Georgia: University of Georgia Press, pp. 58–77.

Wæver, O. (2007). Still a Discipline after All These Debates? In Dunne, T., Kurki, M., and Smith, S. (eds.), *International Relations Theories: Discipline and Diversity.* Oxford: Oxford University Press, pp. 288–308.

Warburton, R. and Kanabar, V. (2012). *The Art and Science of Project Management.* London: RW-Press.

Warner, M. (2003). Styles of Intellectual Publics. In J. Culler and K. Lamb, *Just Being Difficult? Academic Writing in the Public Arena* (p. 116). Stanford, CA: Stanford University Press.

Weaver, P. (2007). The Origins of Modern Project Management. Fourth Annual PMI College of Scheduling Conference 15–18 April 2007. Vancouver: Mosaic Project Services Pty Ltd, pp. 1–23.

Wenger, E. (1998, June). CoP: best practices. Retrieved December 10, 2011 from Communities of Practice. Learning as a social system: www.co-i-l.com/coil/knowledge-garden/cop/lss.shtml.

Westland, A. (2003). *Project Management Lifecycle.* London: Kogan Rage Limited.

Wheatley, M. J. (1999). *Leadership and the New Science: Discovering Order in a Chaotic World.* San Francisco: Berrett-Koehler Publishers.

Whetten, D. (2005). On the meaning of organizational in organizational studies: the case of organizational identity. *Journal of Management Inquiry* 14(1), 13.

White, D. and Fortune, J. (2002). Current practice in project management – an empirical study. *International Journal of Project Management* (20), 1–11.

Willett, F. (1971). *African Art: An Introduction.* New York: Thames and Hudson.

Williams, R. (1958) *Culture and Society.* Harmondsworth: Penguin.

Williams, R. (1961) *The Long Revolution.* Harmondsworth: Penguin.

Wintle, M. (1996). Introduction: Cultural Diversity and Identity in Europe. In M. Wintle (ed.), *Culture and Identity in Europe.* Aldershot: Avebury.

Wolff, T. (1992). Coalition building: one path to empowered communities. Retrieved July 19, 2013 from Tom Wolff & Associates: creating collaborative solutions: www.tomwolff.com/resources/path_to_empowered.pdf.

Yúdice, G. (2003). *The Expediency of Culture: Uses of Culture in the Global Era.* Durham, NC: Duke University Press.

Index